WE ARE
Beloved

A
Lenten
Journey
with
Protestant
Prayer Beads

Kristen E. Vincent

UPPER
ROOM BOOKS®
NASHVILLE

Cover design: Bruce Gore | GoreStudio.com
Typesetting and interior design: PerfecType | Nashville, TN

Library of Congress Cataloging-in-Publication Data

Names: Vincent, Kristen E., author.
Title: We are beloved : a Lenten journey with Protestant prayer beads / Kristen E. Vincent.
Description: Nashville : Upper Room Books, 2019.
Identifiers: LCCN 2018059860 (print) | ISBN 9780835818933 (print)
Subjects: LCSH: Lent—Prayers and devotions. | Beads—Religious aspects—Christianity.
Classification: LCC BV85 .V47 2019 (print) | LCC BV85 (ebook) | DDC
    242/.34—dc23
LC record available at https://lccn.loc.gov/2018059860
LC ebook record available at https://lccn.loc.gov/2019980044

Printed in the United States of America

To all the beloved.
And especially to those who don't realize they are beloved.
Yet.

"Being the Beloved expresses the core truth
of our existence."
—Henri J. M. Nouwen

CONTENTS

INTRODUCTION

The Christian life is a journey. This journey begins with the Word who is with God and who is God—the Word through whom everything comes into being and without whom nothing comes into being, the Word who is life and light for all people.

The journey continues as the Word comes to earth in the form of a tiny baby, wrapped in cloth and lying in a rough-hewn trough, surrounded by loving parents, sleepy livestock, terrified shepherds, and a host of angels.

Our journey goes on as we watch that baby grow into a boy, who will one day scare the living daylights out of his parents when he decides to ditch them. Three days later, they find him teaching in the Temple. Later, that boy will become a young adult. We aren't told much about that time in his life, but we know one day he will show up at a river and ask his cousin John to baptize him. This event turns out to be a key point in our journey.

But let's back up a bit. Let's go back to that sweet little baby whose name is Jesus.

Luke tells us that Jesus "grew and became strong, filled with wisdom; and the favor of God was upon him" (Luke 2:40). As a lifelong churchgoer, I'm familiar with this verse but never gave it much thought. That changed in January 2018.

One of my favorite contemporary theologians is Father Richard Rohr, a Franciscan priest and author who runs the Center for Action and Contemplation in Albuquerque, New Mexico. More than once, Father Richard has written something that has stunned me into silence and invited me into a deeper sense of God's presence. In his daily meditation on January 14, 2018, entitled "God's Self-Revelation," Father Richard explains how God reveals God's self through Jesus Christ. Referencing Luke 2:40, he writes the following:

> It is important to note that Jesus was not born fully mature . . . . He fully entered into the human journey. Many want to imagine that Jesus lying in the manger knew everything from the beginning (which would make his faith a mere caricature, and he would not be the "pioneer and perfecter of our faith" as stated in Hebrews 12:2).[1]

I had to read that several times. I came back to it the next day and again the day after. I realized I'm one of the "many" Father Richard writes about: I'd always assumed that sweet little baby knows he is God right from the start, knows his plan for ministry, and knows how his life on earth will play out. Of course he does.

But what if he doesn't?

This question took me back to my early church history classes in seminary. I had been fascinated by the stories of what life was like in the first three centuries following Christ's resurrection: how the disciples had to process and make sense of what they had just observed, learned, and experienced in Jesus; how they got busy sharing these stories and teachings, spreading the good news, and building the church. I delighted in the stories of how they broke bread together, ministered to the poor, welcomed all who would come, and baptized new converts. What an exciting time this must have been!

But it also was a dangerous time for the early church. The Roman emperor had declared Christianity illegal and insisted that everyone worship the Roman gods to maintain social and political order. Gathering to worship Jesus Christ could put some early Christians at risk of arrest, persecution, and even death. To be safe, most Christians met secretly in their homes or in catacombs—underground passageways and tombs just outside the cities.

As a result, church leaders were unable to hold conferences and meetings to discuss what it meant to be the church. This was significant; any new movement needs time to develop its identity, purpose, message, membership, and practices. The early church needed to determine its Bible—what books it would consider sacred and part of its official canon—what its theology and belief system looked like, what comprised its prayer and worship life, and its membership qualifications—the largest question being whether Jesus followers must convert to Judaism. But such discussions could not take place out in the open. Not surprisingly, a wide variety of theology and practice developed during this time, including some heresies.

One heresy called Arianism taught that Jesus was created by God and thus was not actually divine and had not always existed. Another, called Docetism, taught just the opposite: Jesus only appeared to be human and didn't really suffer and die. As you can imagine, these and other theological differences posed a real problem to the church as it attempted to define and disseminate who and what Christianity was about.

In 312 CE, following his mother's conversion, Roman Emperor Constantine decriminalized Christianity; a year later, he declared Christianity the official religion of the Roman Empire. Finally, the church had the freedom and public space it needed to define its theology and contend with heresies. In 325 CE, church leaders from around the empire gathered for their first official conference in Nicaea, a city in modern-day Turkey. While the leaders addressed many issues—including when to celebrate Easter, how to handle heresies and schisms, and which liturgical practices to adopt—their primary focus was on answering one question: Who was and is Jesus Christ? After much discussion, some angry exchanges, and a good deal of wordsmithing, the Council issued the Nicene Creed, the church's first official statement of faith. Among many points in the Creed, the Council wanted to shut down the heresies about Christ and establish that Jesus was and is *fully divine* by declaring that he is

> eternally begotten of the Father, God from God, Light from Light, true God from true God, begotten, not made, of one Being with the Father. Through him all things were made.

In other words, Christ is one with God, has always existed, and is the source of Creation.

The Creed also affirms that Jesus was *fully human*:

> For us and for our salvation he came down from heaven: by the power of the Holy Spirit he became incarnate from the Virgin Mary, and was made man. For our sake he was crucified under Pontius Pilate; he suffered death and was buried.

Jesus was born in human form from a human mother, he suffered, and he died. Birth, suffering, and death: These are the realities, the effects, of being human. With the Nicene Creed, Christ's divine nature and human nature were declared without reservation. The church took a critical step in formalizing its beliefs and establishing what it means to be a Christ follower.

After reading Father Richard's meditation, I realized I find it easy to profess that Jesus is fully divine. I don't doubt that Jesus Christ is God, one person of the Holy Trinity. He is the Word, the Son of God, the Messiah, the One who became incarnate and was resurrected, ascended into heaven, and who will come again to save the world. Done. But what about when I profess that Jesus is fully human? He was born human, he grew up, he ate and drank and walked this earth, and he suffered and died a horrendous death. But what does that mean?

A human baby knows almost nothing at birth, aside from when she is hungry, wet, not feeling well, too cold or too hot, or tired. She is completely vulnerable, entirely helpless. She has not yet learned to walk and talk and feed herself, to interact with others and express herself. Along the way, she will learn who she is.

Was that true for Jesus too? If we believe he entered fully into the human experience, then apparently so. We return to the verse where Luke says that Jesus "grew in strength and wisdom." We can glean from this statement that Jesus developed just as any other young child. I imagine he experienced scraped knees and hurt feelings; I imagine he pouted when things didn't go his way. As he got older and studied carpentry from his father, I'm sure he made his share of mistakes. It seems that he was respected in the Temple, but he may have endured more than one ribbing from friends who teased him about knowing the scriptures so well. He must have learned how to handle good-natured jokes and navigate social relationships. I wonder if there was a point where he began to notice something different about himself. Did he have any clue about his divinity?

Who knows? Jesus' personhood is all mystery; we cannot understand completely what it means to be fully human and fully divine. We are not meant to. All we can do is have faith in God and be open to Jesus' teachings and the movements of the Holy Spirit as we learn who we are and how we are called to live.

Jesus' full humanity is an essential point of our Christian faith. God becoming incarnate—taking on human flesh—is a fulfillment of Old Testament prophecy. It means that God values the human experience enough that God would experience it by becoming human. The Incarnation means that God loves us enough to want to fully redeem us—offering forgiveness of sin and the gift of eternal life—by living and dying as we do.

I think for the most part, we get all of that. But we may not fully recognize the other benefit of God becoming human: Jesus experienced the human condition in all its highs and lows. He had to figure out things and learn what it means to be human. This means I can look to Jesus for guidance, insight, and encouragement as I navigate the road of life. Because Jesus was fully human, I know he understands the joys and sorrows of human existence. He experienced firsthand what it means to deal with temptation, to weep over suffering and death, to be afraid, and even to doubt our faith. When I'm praying to him about my trials and tribulations, I know he can empathize and offer the comfort and peace I need. When I struggle in my faith, I'm invited to turn to the "pioneer and perfecter of our faith" for wisdom and guidance. When I am suffering, I am drawn to seek solace from the One who has intimate knowledge of suffering and death.

Father Richard also helped me begin to understand that Jesus can encourage me when I do not feel beloved. In the same daily meditation, Father Richard goes on to say, "At Jesus' baptism in the River Jordan, we witness Jesus' dawning realization of who he is: God's 'beloved son.'"[2] Again, this experience is beyond my comprehension, but I know for sure that it is game-changing. It is one thing to follow a Jesus who was always aware of his belovedness; it's an entirely different thing to follow the Jesus who had to learn he was beloved. If Jesus was truly human, there was a time in Jesus' life when he did not consciously know this truth. It means there was a point when he received news of his belovedness and had to spend time sitting with this message before he could accept, own, and live out his belovedness. This realization of Jesus' transformation is life-saving and life-giving for me. When I am not feeling beloved, I can look to the Beloved Son for reminders of who I am and for the way back to my truth.

This journey is about learning and claiming our true identity as beloved. As I shared in my book *Beads of Healing: Prayer, Trauma, and Spiritual Wholeness*, I am a trauma survivor who spent a great deal of her life doubting that she was beloved. I believed that bad things only happen to bad people, not to people God really loves. Therefore, I reasoned, God must not really love me. Through a gradual, often maddeningly slow process, I learned how to be still and listen for God's presence. In the stillness, I began to speak my truth, sharing the full depth of my grief, anger, shame, and fear with God, and I realized that God was listening, sitting with me in my pain, and grieving with me. Slowly, I began to feel how deeply God loves me. More to the point, I learned that God did not cause my trauma, nor was I traumatized because God didn't love me. Indeed, God had been with me through every second of my trauma, suffering with me and helping me survive. Now, God was leading me toward a place of trust, love, gratitude, and forgiveness. In that place I recognized my belovedness. I finally felt and owned that I am God's beloved, and in that moment, I realized there was a place within me—I would call it my soul—that had always known and never once doubted my belovedness.

We live in a world where bad things happen to good people. All of us have pain in our lives, to varying degrees. Our pain has a way of drowning out the sound of our truth, that place deep within us that always has known we are God's beloved. This means the spiritual life is, in part, about recovering our voice and returning to our truth. It's a journey forward and a journey back: forward toward the voice of the One who made us, back to the truth that always has been in us. We clear away the mess of the lies and noise that tell us we are not worthy until we can see with great clarity that we are God's beloved.

Jesus will be our guide for this sacred journey; no other guide will do. Jesus is God who loves us enough to come down to earth and walk hand-in-hand with us through our pain and questions. Jesus willingly took on the pain of the world, enduring betrayal, torture, and a cruel death. Jesus knows the route to recover our truth because Jesus has traversed it. In this book, we will follow him through his faith journey from the moment of his baptism to the moment of his resurrection. We will be with Jesus when God declares that he is God's Beloved Son, and we will follow where that leads him. We will shield our eyes from the blinding light of his transfiguration and ponder what this miracle means. We will watch as Jesus embodies the characteristics of belovedness— passion, healing, service, and courage—in his ministry. We will sit at the foot of the cross as Jesus doubts his belovedness. And on that joyful Easter morning, we will shout "Alleluia!" as we witness his resurrection—the ultimate, life-giving sign of his belovedness. Along the way, we will realize that we too are beloved and called to live life as such.

While it's always a good time to make this journey, Lent provides a particularly appropriate backdrop for it. As Christians, we often review Jesus' life as we prepare for his death and resurrection, and Jesus' death and resurrection are at the heart of our belovedness. Jesus dies to show us just how beloved we are, and Jesus is resurrected to reveal there is no end to our belovedness. We have been God's beloved since before time, and we will continue to be God's beloved beyond the end of time.

I should note that, like all good journeys, this one will be a bit circuitous. To provide a framework for this study, I'm using the texts for Year B of the Revised Common Lectionary, though this study can be used any time. (The lectionary is a list of weekly scripture readings used by a wide number of Protestant churches in the United States and Canada. It's broken up into three cycles that provide a way of reading the majority of the Bible over a three-year period.) The lesson

for Ash Wednesday will provide an overview and founda-
tion for the journey and includes events that occur after
Jesus' baptism. We will then focus on the baptismal story—
the tipping point of our journey—for the First Sunday in
Lent and follow Jesus' journey from there.

Our devotional practices will feed us on our journey.
Each week we will read a Gospel lesson and contemplate its
message. A series of reflection questions will help us ponder
the message of the scripture passage for us personally. We
may use a journal in which to write answers to these questions and to consider how God is speaking to us through
the lesson.

We also will use prayer beads to help quiet our minds and
increase our sense of God's presence. Each lesson includes a
prayer bead experience, a step-by-step devotion using prayer
beads. The experience is designed to help us reflect on the
lesson in a deeper way. Each week also includes a listening meditation, a short phrase meant to be repeated with
each bead aloud or silently. By repeating the meditation,
we will quiet our minds so that we can hear God calling
us "beloved." The beauty of the listening meditation is that
we can continue to repeat it even when we don't have our
prayer beads with us. We can recite it as we're walking the
dog, doing the dishes, going for a run, or driving to work.
We can use it as a breath prayer, inhaling and exhaling as we
say it, to relax and connect our prayer with our body. We

can say it as we lie in bed in the morning before we rise or as we're going to sleep. In this way, we'll not only practice stillness in a variety of settings but also enable the words to seep into our bones and our consciousness to the point that we embody and believe them.

For those who are new to using prayer beads, I have included a brief introduction to Protestant prayer beads at the back of the book. For those who do not own a set of prayer beads, a set can be purchased or made using the instructions provided in the back of the book. However, a set of prayer beads is not necessary to complete this study. We can read the lessons and pray the prayers included in the prayer bead experience without beads.

Some advice as we walk the path toward Easter: Like any journey, we'll want to pay attention. There will be areas that are difficult to navigate because most of us resist the message that we are beloved to some degree. May we be aware of any signs that we are struggling: avoiding this study for any reason, having difficulty focusing, or hearing this message for other people but not owning it for ourselves. When we notice these or other signs of resistance, we shouldn't judge or berate ourselves. Overcoming childhood messages, cultural cues, and any other baggage takes time and effort. Trust me, I know the path well. Judging and berating distract us from recognizing the Holy Spirit's speaking to us. We only can keep showing up and doing what we can. May we focus on the path before us. Better yet, may we focus on Jesus, our guide. He will lead us to our place of truth.

Join me on this journey of belovedness. It is the journey of a lifetime, the journey for which we have been created. And it is a journey without an ending because God's love for us is eternal. We are and will always be God's beloved, forever and ever. Praise be to the God of deep love. Amen.

ASH
WEDNESDAY

THE WAY OF
THE BELOVED

"Be careful that you don't practice your religion in front of people to draw their attention. If you do, you will have no reward from your Father who is in heaven. Whenever you give to the poor, don't blow your trumpet as the hypocrites do in the synagogues and in the streets so that they may get praise from people. I assure you, that's the only reward they'll get. But when you give to the poor, don't let your left hand know what your right hand is doing so that you may give to the poor in secret. Your Father who sees what you do in secret will reward you. When you pray, don't be like hypocrites. They love to pray standing in the synagogues and on the street corners so that people will see them. I assure you, that's the only reward they'll get. But when you pray, go to your room, shut the door, and pray to your Father who is present in that secret place. Your Father who sees what you do in secret will reward you. . . . And when you fast, don't put on a sad face like the hypocrites. They distort their faces so people will know they are fasting. I assure you that they have their reward. When you fast, brush your hair and wash your face. Then you won't look like you are fasting to people, but only to your Father who is present in that secret place. Your Father who sees in secret will reward you. Stop collecting treasures for your own benefit on earth, where moth and rust eat them and where thieves break in and steal them. Instead, collect treasures for yourselves in heaven, where moth and rust don't eat them and where thieves don't break in and steal them. Where your treasure is, there your heart will be also."

—Matthew 6:1-6, 16-21 (CEB)

JESUS HOLDS BACK NOTHING in today's passage. He takes to task those who are showy about their religion. Tooting our own horn when we do something nice for the down-and-out? Knock it off. Praying in a way that is obvious and calls attention to ourselves? Just stop. Making a dramatic show of how miserable we are as we fast? Get over it. Jesus has neither time nor patience for any of this. At least, that's one way of understanding this text; it's certainly the way I've heard it interpreted for most of my life.

What if there's another way? What if Jesus isn't being judgmental? Sure, he's steering us away from these behaviors. He clearly is saying that these practices are problematic and not in our best interest. But what if his tone is not one of criticism?

Let's read the passage again. People blowing trumpets as they give to the poor or standing on a street corner to pray? Sounds a little dramatic, right? Perhaps, as biblical commentator Matt Skinner suggests, Jesus is not speaking literally. Now that I think about it, I can't imagine someone dropping his tithe into the collection plate and then cueing up the brass band. Skinner suggests that perhaps Jesus is being funny. He's using these over-the-top illustrations to show people how silly all of this looks.[3]

I love the thought of Jesus using humor. Funny Jesus makes me smile. This passage occurs early on in his ministry. Not long before, Jesus is baptized, spends time in the desert, and then begins recruiting his disciples. This passage is part of one of his earliest sermons, and Jesus is not wasting any time establishing himself as someone who is not only wise and prophetic but also approachable, witty, and personable.

The over-the-top, showy behaviors that Jesus describes all focus on getting attention. If we brag about helping the poor or draw attention to the fact that we pray or fast, we are seeking attention for ourselves. We are hoping people will notice and be impressed or like us better. Aside from the fact that such a need for attention is driven by low self-esteem, the problem is that we are seeking the wrong kind of attention from the wrong source. It's not other people whose attention we need; it's God's. As Jesus warns in verses 19-21, earthly treasures—including others' approval—won't last.

Going about service, prayer, and fasting in this way misses the point of these practices, which is connection with God. When we minister to those in need, we respond to the presence of God in others and remember the moments when God ministered to us in our need. When we pray, we respond to God's call to step out of the constant hustle of our daily lives, enter into sacred space, and be renewed by God's Spirit. When we fast from food, drugs, technology, or possessions, we let go of the things that cloud our senses so that we can see God for who God is: the God who loves us deeply. The God who calls us beloved—that's the real treasure.

This passage is part of the Sermon on the Mount. It follows the powerful Beatitudes in which Jesus presents a view of God's kingdom that is not based on the earthly need for power and control. Instead, God's kingdom is based in love, compassion, and justice. Jesus reveals that God is a God of deep love who wants the best for all of us. And with today's passage, Jesus shows us how to experience meaningful connection with God and one another. That's why he takes time to teach us the Lord's Prayer (see Matthew 6:7-15).

For most of my life, I thought that God loved me. The key word is *thought*. Intellectually, I knew that God loved me, but my heart didn't believe it. Not really. I didn't feel God's love. I didn't trust it. I didn't feel worthy of it. My pain and childhood trauma led me to believe that God must not care much about me. I know I'm not alone. Many of us who talk a good game when it comes to God's love for us don't believe at our core that we are God's beloved. I think doubting God's love is part of the human condition; so many feel unworthy of it.

Still, whether we believe it or not, we are God's beloved. Deep within us, down deep in our soul, we know this truth. But time, experience, culture, trauma, and other factors slowly cause us to disconnect from this truth and forget who we are. The further we get from our core truth, the more we live as people who are unloved, succumbing to addiction, self-loathing, suicide, prejudice, bullying, gun violence, war, ecological destruction, and so on. That's why this journey is so critical. Our world is desperate to know it is beloved, but that will happen only one person at a time. In other words, this journey begins with us. Once we know we are beloved, we can help others recognize their belovedness. Then those persons will pay it forward and so on.

For the journey to be possible, however, we must reconnect with Love itself. This connection requires a willingness to be present, still, and vulnerable. While this way of being may sound simple and lovely, for most people—myself included—it is quite challenging. Stillness is not so much about keeping our bodies still; the type of stillness I'm talking about involves creating stillness in our mind so that we can focus on our heart. This form of attention can be tricky. Our minds wander. We create grocery lists and to-do reminders, rehash recent interactions, and think about the movie we saw last night. The stillness can feel threatening as it creates space for the memories and feelings we've worked hard to forget or drown out. So, even though we love the idea of prayer, meditation, and other forms of stillness with God, we often avoid them, choosing instead to stay busy or connected to technology. I get it. More importantly, Jesus gets it.

That's why Jesus invites us to these practices as a way of connecting to Love. When we can be still, we can recognize that God is with us. We realize we are not alone with our frenzied thoughts and obsessions and fears and grief. We do not have to deal with our painful memories on our own. God has always been with us, and God is with us now. God is bigger than our pain, regrets, and baggage. When we find moments of true connection with God, we will feel safe, held, healed, and deeply loved. This is the way of the beloved.

Jesus models this type of connection so well. Throughout his ministry, Jesus repeatedly steps out of the hustle and away from his disciples and the crowds to spend time alone with God. I imagine he doesn't make a big show of doing so but rather politely excuses himself and shares that he needs to go away to pray. He does not say this to brag but to model the practice. Then he retreats to a place of silence and solitude where he can experience deep, meaningful connection with his Father. He too needs to be held and healed by the Father. Even as the Beloved Son, he too needs reminders of his belovedness.

As we begin this journey, I encourage engaging in the spiritual practice of stillness. For those who are comfortable with stillness, keep practicing. For those who find stillness difficult or threatening, start small. Practice this week's prayer bead experience or focus on the listening meditation throughout the day. When the mind wanders, just notice it and return to the stillness. When the mind wanders again, notice it and return to the stillness. Repeat as often as necessary. If a particular thought or worry dominates the mind in stillness, welcome it and sit with it. Imagine sitting with God, and see God holding that memory or feeling. Recognize that we are not alone in our pain and that God has the power to transform that pain into healing. On the first day, we may only find it possible to be still for thirty seconds. On the second day, try forty-five seconds. The next day, a little longer. On days that feel like a real struggle, we can offer ourselves grace and try again the next day. On days when stillness feels available and restful, we can offer God gratitude, sink into the stillness, and be renewed.

No matter what, follow the way of the beloved. The path will never fail us. And it will increasingly lead us to awareness of the presence of God—the God who calls us beloved.

REFLECTION QUESTIONS

1. How did the passage from Matthew 6 sound to you when you first read it? What did you hear in Jesus' tone? How does it sound to you now?

2. Have you ever considered that Jesus might be funny? In what ways does that ring true for you? How does this change your reading of this text? In what other instances in scripture might Jesus be using humor to make his point?

3. What is Jesus saying to you about your own devotional practices? When have you engaged in devotional practices to seek others' attention? How is Jesus calling you to deeper, richer connection with God?

4. Do you believe you are God's beloved? Why or why not?

5. According to the author, the way of the beloved is stillness. How do you feel about stillness? Is stillness easy or difficult for you? How will stillness help you claim your belovedness?

6. In the introduction, the author shared Father Richard Rohr's quote about Jesus as the basis for this study (page 8). Do you agree that Jesus wasn't born fully mature, needed to grow in wisdom, and had to learn of his identity as God's Beloved Son? Why or why not? What difference does this make to you? How does this impact your faith?

7. What do you hope to get out of this study? Where do you see connections between the author's experience of accepting her belovedness and your own?

PRAYER BEAD EXPERIENCE

Cross: God of love,

Invitatory bead: who invites me to this journey

Resurrection bead: with your Beloved Son,

1st cruciform bead: open my heart to accept your invitation.

Week beads, set 1: Use each bead to listen for God's call and to respond.

2ⁿᵈ cruciform bead: Hear my concerns about this journey.

Week beads, set 2: Use each bead to offer any concerns you may have about this journey and this study (such as concerns about being still, letting go of the need for others' attention, reasons for doubting your belovedness).

3ʳᵈ cruciform bead: Help me to learn the way of the beloved.

Week beads, set 3: Use each bead to ask for God's guidance in developing a comfort level with stillness or in learning how to go deeper in your practice of stillness.

4ᵗʰ cruciform bead: Let me know I am beloved.

Week beads, set 4: Use each bead to listen for God calling you "beloved."

Resurrection bead: In the name of Jesus,

Invitatory bead: who reveals the way to your heart.

Cross: Amen.

LISTENING MEDITATION

Help me to be still, Lord.

BELOVED WONDER

In those days Jesus came from Nazareth of Galilee and was baptized by John in the Jordan. And just as he was coming up out of the water, he saw the heavens torn apart and the Spirit descending like a dove on him. And a voice came from heaven, "You are my Son, the Beloved; with you I am well pleased." And the Spirit immediately drove him out into the wilderness. He was in the wilderness for forty days, tempted by Satan; and he was with the wild beasts; and the angels waited on him. Now after John was arrested, Jesus came to Galilee, proclaiming the good news of God, and saying, "The time is fulfilled, and the kingdom of God has come near; repent, and believe in the good news."

—Mark 1:9-15

THIS STORY MARKS THE first time we meet Jesus all grown up. Matthew and Luke describe his birth in great detail. Luke briefly recounts the time when Jesus is twelve and, like any preteen boy, ditches his parents, who search frantically until they find him learning in the Temple. Now, suddenly, we have fast-forwarded to Jesus in adulthood.

All four Gospels chronicle the story of Jesus' baptism. From them we can glean the following details about this event:

- By this time, the John we know in the Bible as John the Baptist has been baptizing people for a while. When religious leaders confront him, John explains he is baptizing people with water as a way of getting people ready for the Lamb of God, the Messiah, the one foretold by Hebrew prophets. He emphasizes that the Messiah will baptize with the Holy Spirit and fire and that people should prepare for his coming by repenting and leading a clean life. (See John 1:19-34; Matthew 3:1-12.)

- John's preaching is so effective that people, including religious leaders, come out in droves to be baptized. (See Matthew 3:5-7.)

- Jesus comes to John while "everyone was being baptized" (Luke 3:21, CEB), so there is a crowd present at Jesus' baptism.

- When Jesus asks John to baptize him, John protests that he is unworthy to untie Jesus' sandals, much less baptize him. Still, Jesus insists it's necessary "to fulfill all righteousness" (Matt. 3:15, CEB).

So John baptizes Jesus in the Jordan River. As Jesus comes up out of the water, heaven splits open, the Holy Spirit descends looking like a dove, and a voice from heaven addresses Jesus, saying, "You are my Son, the Beloved; with you I am well pleased."

I cannot imagine what it would have been like to witness this scene. Clearly, it would have been awesome, in the truest sense of the word. Would it also have been a little terrifying? Would I have understood what was happening?

I wonder what it must be like for Jesus. God claims Jesus as God's Son and calls him Beloved. How does this make Jesus feel? I would guess that Jesus experiences a mix of joy, surprise, bewilderment, and confusion. I suspect this because Jesus is fully human, and that would be a very human response to hearing such a divine proclamation.

Clearly Jesus needs time to process this news because the scripture reading tells us that as soon as Jesus hears that he is the Beloved, "the Spirit forced Jesus out in the wilderness" (Mark 1:12, CEB). Isn't that interesting? Jesus experiences this tremendous, awesome event, and immediately he is sent out to the desert. For forty days he struggles. He is hungry and lonely and tired. He comes across wild animals and is tempted by Satan. The fact that this wilderness experience immediately follows the voice from God tells me that Jesus needs time for stillness to figure out what it means to be God's Beloved. He needs time to question it, fight it, and try it on for size. He needs to spend time in wonder before he can own it.

After forty days in the wilderness, Jesus finally reaches a place where he can own his identity as God's Beloved. How do we know? Because the very next verses tell us that Jesus goes into Galilee "announcing God's good news . . . 'Change your hearts and lives, and trust this good news!'" (Mark 1:14-15, CEB).

For me, Jesus' process is very good news. As I shared earlier, I spent a lot of my life not believing I was God's beloved. When I finally heard—*really* understood—that God loves me, I needed time to process that message. Decades of pain, disbelief, anger, and baggage did not disappear in an instant. It took time to sit with the news of my belovedness. I had to share my questions and doubts with God. I had to offer all the reasons I thought I was unloved and unlovable and listen for God's response. Gradually, I began to try living as someone who is beloved. Sometimes that went well, other days not so much. Little by little, I felt more beloved each day, until one day I just knew, believed, and embodied that I am deeply loved by God.

What is the good news that Jesus declares once he owns his belovedness? We too are God's beloved. God is willing to split open the heavens to declare that we are God's beloved children. God wants us to know we bring God much happiness. God calls us to live as people who are beloved. From Jesus, we learn that once we come to own God's deep love for us, we cannot help but want to share that news with others. We feel compelled to help others recognize and own God's deep love for themselves.

This feeling of belovedness doesn't come easily to us. We are surrounded by media, cultural norms, and even religious folks who tell us that we are not enough or are too much of something. We are told that we must earn love by being good or pretty or smart or that we are sinful and unworthy of so much. It is good news to know that no matter who we are or what we have done—no matter what anyone thinks or says—we are beloved by God. Because God is Love.

Say it aloud: God. Is. Love.

God created us in God's image, which means we reflect divine love. God created us for love. And God created us to be love. We are beloved. As Henri Nouwen writes, "Being the Beloved expresses the core truth of our existence."[4] Love is who we are. It is our truth. And nothing can erase that truth.

We're going to need time to wonder, to ponder, and to own this core truth of our existence. It won't come quickly or all at once. But that's okay. Jesus needed time to figure it out too. Throughout this time, "the angels took care of him" (Mark 1:13, CEB). They'll take care of us too until we finally revel in our belovedness. At that point, we won't be able to help it. We'll want to share the good news.

REFLECTION QUESTIONS

1. Does it help you to know that Jesus had to learn that he was beloved and what it means to be beloved? If so, how is it helpful? How can Jesus help you on your journey?

2. What do you think of the idea that Jesus' time in the wilderness was, in part, about his need to wrestle with the idea of being beloved? How did he use that time to be still and own this truth? How can you do the same?

3. What does it mean to you that you are God's beloved? When have you struggled to believe in this part of your identity?

4. Who are the angels who are helping you in the wilderness as you are learning to be beloved?

5. At this point in time, where do you see yourself in the story: in the moment of God declaring you beloved, in the wilderness, or beginning to share the good news?

6. Consider Henri Nouwen's quote on page 35. Do you believe that belovedness is the core truth of your

existence? Why or why not? If not, what is keeping you from believing that?

7. How have you practiced stillness this week? What have you noticed?

Prayer Bead Experience

Cross: God of love,

Invitatory bead: who declared Jesus

Resurrection bead: to be your Beloved Son,

1st cruciform bead: you find such happiness in Jesus.

Week beads, set 1: Use each bead to listen to the love and joy in God's voice as God declares Jesus to be beloved.

2nd cruciform bead: I too am your beloved.

Week beads, set 2: Use each bead to listen to the love and joy in God's voice as God declares you to be beloved. Take your time, and revel in this experience.

3rd cruciform bead: Guide me on this journey as I learn to accept my belovedness. In particular, help me when I do not believe it or when I resist it.

Week beads, set 3: Use each bead to pray for guidance, strength, and angels to support you in the wilderness when you are not feeling beloved and as you are learning to live beloved.

4ᵗʰ cruciform bead: Lead me to a place where I can share the good news of my belovedness with the world and help others recognize their own belovedness.

Week beads, set 4: Use each bead to imagine what it will look and feel like when you have owned your belovedness to the point that you are able to share it with others. Pray for guidance and patience on your journey toward owning and sharing your belovedness.

Resurrection bead: In the name of Jesus,

Invitatory bead: your Beloved Son.

Cross: Amen.

LISTENING FOCUS

I am beloved.

SECOND
SUNDAY IN
LENT

BELOVED LISTENING

Six days later Jesus took Peter, James, and
John, and brought them to the top of a very
high mountain where they were alone. He
was transformed in front of them, and his
clothes were amazingly bright, brighter than
if they had been bleached white. Elijah and
Moses appeared and were talking with Jesus.
Peter reacted to all of this by saying to Jesus,
"Rabbi, it's good that we're here. Let's make
three shrines—one for you, one for Moses, and
one for Elijah." He said this because he didn't
know how to respond, for the three of them
were terrified. Then a cloud overshadowed
them, and a voice spoke from the cloud, "This
is my Son, whom I dearly love. Listen to him!"
Suddenly, looking around, they no longer saw

anyone with them except Jesus. As they were
coming down the mountain, he ordered them
not to tell anyone what they had seen until
after the Human One had risen from the dead.

—Mark 9:2-9 (CEB)

I GET IT. IF I were on that mountain with Jesus and Peter,
James, and John, I would be pretty freaked out too. Jesus is
glowing! His clothes have turned whiter than the whitest
white. Moses and Elijah have shown up and started chatting
with him. This is no ordinary day. The disciples have no
idea what is going on. They cannot explain it; no words can
describe this experience. They have no idea what to think
or what to feel. So Peter offers to build three dwellings.

I get it. I would do the same thing.

Building is active. It would give the disciples something
to do. They could design and gather and saw and hammer.
They could take the energy from this other-worldly experience and channel it into something familiar. They could
feel like they were contributing, like they were in control
of the situation.

I would be right there with them. And when the dwellings were up and I still didn't know what to do, I would
bake and then entertain Jesus and his guests. I would take
selfies and post them to Facebook. #Transfiguration

But Peter doesn't get to build anything because almost as soon as the words are out of his mouth, God breaks into the scene to make things even more mysterious and terrifying. God declares, "This is my Son, whom I dearly love. Listen to him!"

Sound familiar?

It's almost the exact same wording God uses in last week's scripture reading. God again declares Jesus to be God's Beloved Son. But there is one key difference in these two passages from Mark. In the baptism story, God makes a statement to Jesus: "You are my Son, whom I dearly love." In the second, God makes a statement about Jesus: "This is my Son, whom I dearly love." Whereas the first declaration of belovedness is for Jesus' benefit, this one is for ours. Now that Jesus knows he is beloved, God wants to be sure we too understand that Jesus is beloved.

Something else is happening here: Last week we witnessed Jesus being baptized—something that happens to humans—and God's declaring him beloved. This week we are watching Jesus being transfigured—something that only happens to Jesus—and God's declaring him beloved. Jesus is beloved as both human and divine.

Following this declaration, God adds, "Listen to him!"

Listen to him.

That's what the disciples are called to do. That's all any of us is called to do: Listen to Jesus. In listening, we hear who God is—a God who loves us deeply—and we hear who we are—beloved children. We hear our call to love and worship God and to love our neighbors as ourselves. Listening leads us to our belovedness.

Listening may seem simple. Yet when we try to listen, we find that it's much more difficult than we anticipated. We're conditioned to be active—to be and to do. We like to stay busy, plugged in, and in control. We like to produce. But listening requires staying still, unplugging, being patient, and giving up control. When we listen, we may hear something we don't want to hear or are not ready to hear. Perhaps many of us aren't good at listening because listening requires courage.

I like that we read this week's scripture passage after the passage about Jesus' baptism. In watching God confirm Jesus' belovedness a second time, I imagine how God does the same for us. I believe God is willing to repeat it over and over, as often as we need to hear it, until we are convinced of it: We are God's beloved.

These two texts in Mark's Gospel emphasize the need for listening. As we may have begun to figure out in the past week, it's not easy to acknowledge and accept that we are beloved. As great as being beloved sounds, our baggage and cultural messages get in the way of owning this truth for ourselves. It makes us uncomfortable. Like Peter, we'd rather keep busy and stay one step ahead of the doubts and fears that tell us we are anything but beloved. But God calls us to listen for a reason. In the listening, we hear our truth: We are beloved. In the listening, we are healed. In the listening, we begin to understand our belovedness, believe it, and learn how to live into it.

This all takes time. We're spending Lent learning to listen for God calling us beloved. But we'll need more time to sit with this truth, question it, and resist it before we can finally own it. That may be one reason Jesus tells the disciples not to share what they have seen and heard that day. He knows they don't understand what has happened. As Jesus needs forty days in the wilderness, he knows they need time to process their experience and sit with it to begin to understand it before they can share the good news. We'll need to go through those same steps to own our belovedness. We'll need to be patient. We'll need to follow the way of the beloved.

If we can find patience and practice taking time each day to sit and listen to Jesus, then over time we will begin to hear what he is saying to us. We will hear his message of deep love. We will begin to embody it. That's a tremendous thing. Peter doesn't get to build the dwellings just because there's no need for dwellings. Rather, Peter doesn't get to build the dwellings because God calls him to *be* the dwelling. God is calling him to be beloved. And in living into his belovedness, Peter becomes transfigured.

When we begin to embody Jesus' words—when we accept them and begin to live them out—then we will become the dwelling place. We will become the vessel that carries Jesus' message of belovedness to the world. #Transfiguration

Reflection Questions

1. Why do you think Peter offers to build the dwellings? When have you avoided being present to an experience by focusing on another task and staying busy? What is difficult about staying present?

2. Instead of trying to be busy, imagine yourself sitting and watching Jesus' transfiguration. What do you notice? How does it make you feel? How is it overwhelming?

3. Why do you think God declares Jesus the Beloved Son a second time? In what ways does God repeat the news that you are beloved? How many times is God willing to repeat the news of your belovedness until you begin to believe it?

4. In what ways do you listen to Jesus? What makes listening to Jesus difficult? What would make it easier? How can listening to Jesus help you own your belovedness?

5. What does it mean to you to be the dwelling place for Jesus? How does owning your belovedness transfigure

you? What difference will that make for you? for the world?

6. So far, you've read multiple times that belovedness is your core truth and something that your soul has always known. How do you feel about this? What does this mean for you?

7. How have you practiced stillness this week? What have you noticed?

Prayer Bead Experience

Cross: God of love,

Invitatory bead: who reminds us again and again

Resurrection bead: that Jesus is your Beloved Son,

1st cruciform bead: you declared a second time that Jesus is your Beloved Son. Help me to hear as you repeatedly call me beloved.

Week beads, set 1: Use each bead to listen as God calls you beloved over and over again.

2nd cruciform bead: My natural tendency is to check out when something awesome or overwhelming occurs. Help me to stay still and be fully present no matter what.

Week beads, set 2: Use each bead to ask for God's help in staying fully present in the moment, rather than trying to be busy or in control.

3rd cruciform bead: You encourage me to listen to Jesus. Help me to listen to your Son and better understand my belovedness.

Week beads, set 3: Use each bead to hear God calling you to listen to Jesus, and consider what will help you do this.

4th cruciform bead: You invite me to be transfigured in my own way as I come to embody Jesus' message and live as your beloved for the world.

Week beads, set 4: Use each bead to consider what embodying Jesus' message and living as one transformed by God's deep love mean.

Resurrection bead: In the name of Jesus,

Invitatory bead: your Beloved Son.

Cross: Amen.

LISTENING MEDITATION

I am listening.

BELOVED PASSION

It was nearly time for the Jewish Passover, and Jesus went up to Jerusalem. He found in the temple those who were selling cattle, sheep, and doves, as well as those involved in exchanging currency sitting there. He made a whip from ropes and chased them all out of the temple, including the cattle and the sheep. He scattered the coins and overturned the tables of those who exchanged currency. He said to the dove sellers, "Get these things out of here! Don't make my Father's house a place of business." His disciples remembered that it is written, *Passion for your house consumes me.* Then the Jewish leaders asked him, "By what authority are you doing these things? What miraculous sign will you show us?"

Jesus answered, "Destroy this temple and in three days I'll raise it up." The Jewish leaders replied, "It took forty-six years to build this temple, and you will raise it up in three days?" But the temple Jesus was talking about was his body. After he was raised from the dead, his disciples remembered what he had said, and they believed the scripture and the word that Jesus had spoken.

—John 2:13-22 (CEB)

THIS IS THE FIRST time in our study that we are focusing on the Gospel of John. Up to now, we've read primarily from Matthew and Mark, which, along with the Gospel of Luke, are referred to as the Synoptic Gospels. They offer a similar, parallel synopsis of Jesus' life: what he did, where he went, what he said, and so on. John's Gospel is different in many ways, including that rather than offering an overall synopsis of Jesus' life, John focuses on explaining who Jesus is. Right off the bat, John tells us that Jesus "was the Word and the Word was with God and the Word was God. . . . The Word became flesh and made his home among us" (1:1, 14, CEB).

John also records Jesus' seven "I am" statements:

- I am the bread of life (6:35).
- I am the light of the world (8:12).
- I am the gate of the sheep (10:7).

- I am the good shepherd (10:11).
- I am the resurrection and the life (11:25).
- I am the way, the truth, and the life (14:6).
- I am the true vine (15:1).

First and foremost, John wants us to know that Jesus is the Christ, the Messiah, the Son of God, so that we will believe and have eternal life. That's the context for this week's story about Jesus clearing the Temple. In the other Gospels, this event occurs toward the end, after all of Jesus' other teachings and miracles. But John places this story right up front in chapter two. The only events that precede this one are John's description of Jesus as the Word, the story of Jesus' baptism and how Jesus calls his disciples, and the miracle of Jesus turning water into wine.

Then—boom!—Jesus clears the Temple.

John wastes no time in telling this story because it's another illustration of who Jesus is: Jesus is the Temple. "Destroy this temple and in three days I'll raise it up," Jesus says. We understand this statement as a reference to Jesus' crucifixion and resurrection.

But what does this tell us about being beloved?

In pointing to his upcoming death and resurrection, Jesus compares his body to the Jerusalem Temple. The Temple is the holiest of places, the center of Jewish religious life. The Jews have spent decades planning and constructing it and then establishing a wealth of rules and rituals to mark its holiness. John gives us a sense of its significance in the religious leaders' reaction to Jesus' suggestion that they destroy it: What? Are you crazy?

I take Jesus' metaphor to mean that our bodies too are holy places. We are created in God's image. Just as the Jews invest a great deal of time, thought, and resources into building the Temple, God invests a great deal—God's own image—into the creation of our physical bodies, which serve as the vessels for our spirits. Paul writes in 1 Corinthians 6:19-20, "Don't you know that your body is a temple of the Holy Spirit who is in you? Don't you know that you have the Holy Spirit from God, and you don't belong to yourselves? You have been bought and paid for, so honor God with your body" (CEB).

Seeing our bodies as holy may not come easily to us. Even in Jesus' time, there are many rules—particularly for women—that can make it sound as if physical bodies are dirty or defiled. In our time, cultural messages about weight and ability and sexuality and color make it even more difficult to love our bodies. But when we question the holiness of our physical bodies, we need only remember that God becomes human in the form of Jesus and then declares Jesus to be God's Beloved. Part of being beloved is recognizing the sacred value of our bodies and honoring them as such.

This scene in John's Gospel begins with Jesus walking into the Temple and seeing the merchants selling livestock—cattle, sheep, and doves (often the only animal affordable for the poor, particularly women)—that will be used in ritual sacrifices and witnessing the money changers converting Greek and Roman currency into Jewish currency for offerings. Jesus seems to feel that this holy place is being overrun with commercialism, that the focus has become more about profit than worship. That makes him angry, livid even. He unleashes his fury on the unsuspecting merchants, money collectors, and livestock. John is telling us that Jesus is passionate.

Passion doesn't exist in a vacuum. It is intense and derives from deep love or deep anger. Passion, then, must be an inherent part of belovedness since our belovedness is the expression of God's deep love within us. The more in touch we become with our belovedness, the more passionate we become about God and all that God has created. We become passionate about who we are, how we reflect God's sacred image, and who God calls us to be in the world. We become passionate about the world, wanting to care for and nurture other people and all creation. We cannot help but be passionate; it is the result of our belovedness.

Our bodies serve as the vessels for our soul, the place within us that knows unequivocally that we are God's beloved. We connect with our passions within and through our bodies. When I finally began my healing journey and developed a comfort level with stillness, I realized how disconnected I had been from my body. My body held the memories of my trauma and my feelings of shame, which I had worked hard to avoid. But as I practiced being still with God, I learned to reconnect with my body. Through deep breathing, gaining awareness of how my body feels and moves, caring for it, and appreciating its wonder and beauty, I returned to my body. I realized it is not something to be avoided, ignored, or criticized. Rather, my body is part of who I am and thus part of my belovedness.

But this was just the beginning. I learned that my body is chock-full of wisdom. The more I connected with my body, the more I began to trust it. I learned to pay attention to its signals: If I feel tired, then I need rest; if I feel hungry, then I need to eat; if I feel energized, then my body is ready to move. Though these realizations may seem obvious, I was learning for the first time that my body tells me what it needs. So I went deeper. In my time with God, I paid attention to my physical feelings: whether my shoulders were tense or my back hurt, whether I was breathing deeply. I looked for connections between these feelings and my thoughts and prayers. Often, the physical sensations pointed to a deeper spiritual or emotional issue. Recognizing the connection allowed me to lift the underlying issue to God and listen for God's response. Through listening to my body's wisdom in prayer, I've experienced some incredible epiphanies that have helped me work through emotional issues and led me deeper into my calling, into the place of living out the passion of my belovedness.

While finding our passion is a wonderful gift, as we see in our scripture story, passion isn't always viewed favorably. Though Jesus clears the Temple in a passionate desire to honor the sacred space, the merchants, money collectors, and religious leaders are unhappy. The Synoptic Gospels all agree that this event seals Jesus' fate: From this point on, the leaders begin to plot his death. Jesus knows that his passion will ultimately lead to the true Passion.

In other words, passion has consequences. In our passion to live out our belovedness, we may reveal things the world would prefer to keep hidden as we knock against the status quo. In being true to our belovedness, we may end up ostracized or vilified. We may wonder whether it's better to play it safe. But belovedness is not a promise of safety; it is a promise of deep love and new life with Jesus Christ.

This journey is about accepting that we are God's beloved and learning what it means to live as God's beloved, no matter the cost. When I first envisioned this study, I imagined we would explore what it means to pray and worship and serve in community as beloved people. And given that this is a Lenten study, I understood we would eventually get into the topic of sacrifice. I had no idea it would come about so early. But perhaps it's good that we're jumping head first into the deep end and talking about passion now, long before Easter.

Being beloved is no small thing. It is enormous. The God of the universe has declared that we are beloved. The God of all creation has called us forth to live and serve as beloved.

That fact should delight us and inspire us and terrify us all at the same time. That's the nature of passion. It's deep. But we can trust deep. We can trust it because deep within us is the wisdom of our bodies, which knows our capabilities. We can trust it because deep within us are our souls, which know the truth of our belovedness. And we can trust it because we are not alone in the depths. As Psalm 42:7 tells us, "Deep calls to deep." God is with us. Thanks be to God. Amen.

REFLECTION QUESTIONS

1. Why do you think John includes this story of Jesus clearing the Temple so early in his Gospel? What does this story tell you about who Jesus is?

2. Do you believe your body is a temple? Why or why not? How does thinking of your body as the vessel for your soul change the way you view your body? How can you honor your body as a temple?

3. What connection do you see between passion and your body? How can you practice listening to your body to discover your passion?

4. Consider Jesus' passion in the Temple. In what ways does Jesus' being angry and even violent as he overturns

tables and chases away the merchants surprise you? What does this tell you about passion in your own life? about anger?

5. Describe the connection between passion and being beloved in your life. In what ways do you struggle to see this connection? How will you foster it?

6. What would it look like if you lived life fully as God's beloved? What would be the same? What would be different? What would be the consequences?

7. How have you practiced stillness this week? What have you noticed?

PRAYER BEAD EXPERIENCE

Cross: God of love,

Invitatory bead: who sent your Son, Jesus Christ,

Resurrection bead: so that we might know what it's like to live passionately,

1st cruciform bead: help me to believe that my body is a temple and to see it as the vessel for my soul.

Week beads, set 1: Use each bead to recognize how your body is a temple, designed by God to serve as a container for your soul.

2nd cruciform bead: I confess that I don't always honor my body. Help me to do that.

Week beads, set 2: Use each bead to confess the ways in which you have not honored your body as a temple and to consider ways to begin or continue to honor your body.

3rd cruciform bead: I know that as your beloved, I am called to live a passionate life that brings glory to you. Help me to be passionate for the things that glorify you.

Week beads, set 3: Use each bead to begin to recognize the passion within you that comes from being beloved, and to listen for God's guidance in identifying your passion.

4th cruciform bead: Help me to live fully as your beloved, no matter the cost.

Week beads, set 4: Use each bead to discern the areas in which God is calling you to live out your belovedness and to pray for courage to follow through.

Resurrection bead: In the name of Jesus,

Invitatory bead: your Beloved Son.

Cross: Amen.

Listening Meditation

I am passionate.

BELOVED HEALING

"Just as Moses lifted up the snake in the wilderness, so must the Human One be lifted up so that everyone who believes in him will have eternal life. God so loved the world that he gave his only Son, so that everyone who believes in him won't perish but will have eternal life. God didn't send his Son into the world to judge the world, but that the world might be saved through him. Whoever believes in him isn't judged; whoever doesn't believe in him is already judged, because they don't believe in the name of God's only Son. This is the basis for judgment: The light came into the world, and people loved darkness more than light, for their actions are evil. All who do wicked things hate the light and don't come to the

light for fear that their actions will be exposed
to the light. Whoever does the truth comes to
the light so that it can be seen that their actions
were done in God."

—John 3:14-21 (CEB)

THERE'S A LOT GOING on in this week's scripture reading,
and I'll do my best to make sense of it. Not surprisingly, as
we travel closer to the cross, our journey gets a little tougher.
We're going to have to work at this lesson.

Our scripture reading is part of a larger conversation
between Jesus and Nicodemus, a Pharisee, who seems to be
making a sincere effort to understand who Jesus is and how
he can perform miracles. But Jesus doesn't make things easy
for Nicodemus. Each time Nicodemus asks a question, Jesus
responds with a convoluted answer. At the point where we
begin our reading, Jesus is trying to explain eternal life by
referencing a story from the Hebrew scriptures about Moses.

In Numbers 21:4-9, the Israelites are still wandering in
the desert after decades of travel. They've had it. They're
tired, hungry, thirsty, and sick to death of eating manna—the
only food they've had for all these years. So they complain
and accuse God and Moses of bringing them into the desert
for the sole purpose of killing them. God seems to respond
with "If you say so" by sending poisonous snakes to bite the
people. Many of the Israelites die, which leads the people to

issue quick apologies and requests for *immediate* deliverance from the snakes (emphasis my own because snakes).

At this point, God instructs Moses to make a poisonous snake (How does one make a snake? Is there a Pinterest page for DIY reptiles?), place it on a pole, and show it to the people. Anyone who looks at it will be healed.

Jesus uses this story from the Hebrew scriptures to reference his impending crucifixion and resurrection. He explains that in being "lifted up"—in hanging and dying on the cross—he will be like the serpent on the pole: The world will be healed.

It strikes me that the Israelites must look at the pole to be healed from the snake bite. Jesus' analogy implies that people must believe in Jesus to be healed from sin and have eternal life. This statement is so important that Jesus repeats it in one of the most famous and revered verses of the entire Bible: "God so loved the world that he gave his only Son, so that everyone who believes in him won't perish but will have eternal life" (John 3:16, CEB).

I hadn't considered this verse in this way before: We are *invited* to believe in Jesus so that we can have eternal life. Rather than being passively gathered into God's kingdom, we're encouraged to take an active role in our salvation.

I think this invitation tells us something important about being beloved. We are God's beloved; that's our truth, and we cannot change it. No matter what, we always have been, are, and always will be beloved. However, we will enjoy our belovedness when we believe it, when we own it, and when we live into it. The more we recognize our belovedness, the more we will experience its benefits: freedom, richness, joy, and healing. I'm not saying that our belovedness begins only when we accept it; we're beloved no matter what. But we won't experience the true gift of our belovedness until we accept it. We play an active role in owning our belovedness; we choose whether to accept it and how to live out of it.

What happens if we don't accept it? When we deny that we are beloved, we experience judgment. As Jesus explains, God did not send God's Son to judge but to save. But when people choose not to believe God's Son, "they are already judged."

This is where things start to sound harsh. Jesus begins talking about judgment, evil, and wickedness. These statements are familiar to us; they're often used to scare people into going to church and "getting saved." Many fire-and-brimstone Christians have told us that God is going to rain fire upon us in judgment if we don't believe in Jesus.

But that's not how I read this passage. I think Jesus is describing what happens when we do not believe Jesus' message of our belovedness. This is not hard to imagine. When we do not believe that we are beloved, we open ourselves to low self-confidence, self-loathing, fear, and anxiety. As many of us have experienced, such adverse emotions and self-perceptions can lead to a whole host of problems: broken relationships, violence, addiction, alienation, apathy, suicide, murder, poverty, war, ecological devastation, and so on. Thus, contrary to those fire-and-brimstone preachers, judgment and suffering come not from God but from ourselves. We judge ourselves when we determine that we are not worthy of being beloved. We cause our own suffering when we live out of this place of un-belovedness. And so it is vital that we believe Jesus. Our very lives—and the fate of all creation—depend upon it.

For us to care about ourselves, others, and the rest of creation, we must recognize and claim our belovedness. But as we're learning through this study, owning our belovedness is a process. In the end, it's really a process of healing from pain and trauma, healing from the lies and messages we've received and internalized, healing our relationship with our bodies, healing our relationship with others, and, perhaps most importantly, healing our understanding of God.

God could have chosen anything for the Israelites to focus on: a flower, a rainbow, a fluffy bunny. Instead, God chose a snake. Snakes represent so much for us: the serpent that tempted Adam and Eve in the garden of Eden, an animal that is threatening and can inflict great pain, suffering, and even death. I believe this is an apt symbol for talking about healing. While we all want to be healed, few of us are eager to go through the process of healing. Healing is difficult, painful, and messy. Whether our healing requires surgery, multiple rounds of radiation, casts, and physical therapy or working through traumatic memories and long-repressed emotions, healing takes time and effort and, most of all, a lot of courage. In offering up the snake, God is telling us that we will need to face our pain to be healed. It's the only way. God is asking us to be brave. But God is also reminding us that God will be with us in our healing. In the person of Jesus, God is lifted up on the cross for all of us to see, bearing our fears and our heartaches and our sin. God will bear all of this for us and with us. When we focus on the God who brings us to the place of our belovedness, we will be able to heal.

Healing will look different for each person, so I can't offer a prescription. But I can say that healing begins with stillness in the presence of God. If I sound like a broken record at this point, it's with good reason: Recovering the truth of our belovedness begins and ends in stillness. That's where we break through the noise, find God, and discover our truth. That's why stillness is the way of the beloved.

We are each on a journey toward healing to one degree or another. Though I've made incredible progress in my journey of healing from childhood trauma, I am not fully healed from that event and have just begun journeys of healing from other events in my life. And there will be things that happen in the future for which I will need healing.

That's why I return to stillness again and again. I know that I will be able to fulfill my calling only by sitting with God, allowing God to redeem my pain, and being reminded that I am beloved. From there I can practice living as one who is beloved.

When we believe that we are beloved and live as beloved people, we are healed. In turn, we can help others understand they are beloved; then they can be healed. And the world can be healed. This is how we are called into healing: We are participants in God's act of healing the world.

I believe that God could have simplified everything by just making it so that we are born knowing we are beloved. *But where's the fun in that?* God seems to be saying. If that were the case, we might take our belovedness for granted. We'd miss out on the journey and the opportunity to discover and question and test and own and revel in our belovedness. Our journey leads to healing, which leads to gratitude, which leads to praise for the God who created us and calls us beloved. Thanks be to God. Amen.

Reflection Questions

1. How do you understand the analogy between Jesus on the cross and the serpent on a pole?
2. What do you think about Jesus saying that we must believe in him to have eternal life? Why do you think

we are invited to believe? What difference does it make for you to feel invited to take an active role in accepting and owning your belovedness?

3. How do you read Jesus' statements about judgment? In what ways do you agree or disagree with the author's reading of this passage on judgment?

4. How does thinking of judgment as a natural consequence of not believing we are beloved impact your faith? What signs of self-judgment can you recognize in your life? in the world?

5. Where are you in your journey so far? In what ways are you feeling more beloved? In what ways are you struggling to believe you are beloved?

6. Where do you need healing in your life? What does healing look like for you?

7. How have you practiced stillness this week? What have you noticed?

Prayer Bead Experience

Cross: God of love,

Invitatory bead: who lifted up your Beloved Son

Resurrection bead: so that we might be healed,

1st cruciform bead: I do not always believe I am beloved.

Week beads, set 1: Use each bead to confess the ways in which you do not believe you are beloved.

2nd cruciform bead: Help me to see Jesus, your Beloved Son, lifted on the cross and believe that I am beloved.

Week beads, set 2: Use each bead to see Jesus on the cross, to recognize the depth of his love for you as he hung on the cross, and to accept that his sacrifice was to underscore your belovedness.

3rd cruciform bead: Help me see judgment as a sign that I need healing.

Week beads, set 3: Use each bead to sit with the areas where you experience self-judgment or judgment of others, and lift those areas to God for healing.

4th cruciform bead: Help me to reach a point in my belovedness where I seek to help others recognize their belovedness.

Week beads, set 4: Use each bead to consider the ways in which you might help others heal from their own brokenness so they may see they are beloved.

Resurrection bead: In the name of Jesus Christ,

Invitatory bead: your Beloved Son.

Cross: Amen.

Listening Meditation

I am healing.

BELOVED SERVICE

Some Greeks were among those who had come up to worship at the festival. They came to Philip, who was from Bethsaida in Galilee, and made a request: "Sir, we want to see Jesus." Philip told Andrew, and Andrew and Philip told Jesus. Jesus replied, "The time has come for the Human One to be glorified. I assure you that unless a grain of wheat falls into the earth and dies, it can only be a single seed. But if it dies, it bears much fruit. Those who love their lives will lose them, and those who hate their lives in this world will keep them forever. Whoever serves me must follow me. Wherever I am, there my servant will also be. My Father will honor whoever serves me. Now I am deeply troubled. What should I say?

'Father, save me from this time?' No, for this is the reason I have come to this time. Father, glorify your name!" Then a voice came from heaven, "I have glorified it, and I will glorify it again." The crowd standing there heard and said, "It's thunder." Others said, "An angel spoke to him." Jesus replied, "This voice wasn't for my benefit but for yours. Now is the time for judgment of this world. Now this world's ruler will be thrown out. When I am lifted up from the earth, I will draw everyone to me." (He said this to show how he was going to die.)

—John 12:20-33 (CEB)

SOME GREEKS COME TO worship at the festival and ask to see Jesus. It is such a minor detail; yet it seems to be exactly what Jesus has been waiting for.

As Jesus' ministry develops, more people begin following him. But aside from a few folks, he preaches mostly to his fellow Jews. Now, some Greeks have asked to see Jesus. They are not Jews; they are Gentiles. We understand this to mean they represent everyone who is not Jewish. The fact that they are seeking Jesus and wanting to learn from him means that Jesus' message has spread to the Gentiles. His message is spreading not only to the nation of Israel but also to all nations.

Jesus has been hoping for his message to have this type of reach. And I'm guessing he has been fearing it as well. Now that he's sure his message will be received by all nations, he recognizes it is time for him to die. "The time has come for the Human One to be glorified," he says. I imagine this is a bittersweet moment for Jesus. It should be a bittersweet moment for us as well because Jesus goes on to explain that wherever he goes, his servants will be there too. We, his servants, will follow in his footsteps, even when those footsteps lead directly to the cross.

It's okay if that path makes us nervous. Jesus is nervous too. He is deeply troubled and has considered asking God to keep all this from happening. Jesus knows how he will die and how excruciating his death will be. But he doesn't ask God to save him. As God's Beloved Son, Jesus knows his calling is to bring glory to God, even if that's not an easy task. So he remains committed to his journey by saying, "Father, glorify your name!"

God rewards Jesus' faithfulness by breaking into space and time. This is the third time in our beloved journey that we've heard God's voice. In the first two instances, God declares that Jesus is God's Beloved Son. The first time God adds that God delights in Jesus; the second time God encourages us to listen to Jesus. This time, God responds to Jesus' commitment by saying, "I have glorified it, and I will glorify it again."

While God doesn't speak directly to Jesus' belovedness, this statement is another way for God to affirm Jesus' identity in God. Jesus has just confirmed that he will move forward in his journey of beloved servanthood for the sole purpose of glorifying God's name, even though that purpose terrifies him. God seems to be saying, "Well done, my Beloved Son. Your faithfulness and commitment have already brought glory to my name, and your continued faithfulness will glorify it again."

Next week we will watch Jesus enter the gates of Jerusalem, riding a young donkey. He knows he is going to die in Jerusalem, but he goes there anyway, staying true to his calling as God's Beloved Son. There is no greater sign of faithfulness than this. Jesus chooses to serve God faithfully despite the risks, and in so doing, he brings glory to God's name. And that, my friends, is how we live out our belovedness.

I have a friend—we'll call him George—who is a pastor. George is a pacifist; he does not believe there is any purpose in war or violence. Yet he has been serving as an Army chaplain for the last three decades. When I asked him about this seeming contradiction, he described hearing news of the Gulf War. He did not agree with our country's decision to go to war, but he recognized that soldiers would be called upon to fulfill their duty and fight on our behalf. George also understood the costs of their faithful service: Thousands of people would face extremely frightening situations, put themselves at great risk, and possibly die. He knew how traumatic this would be and how afraid they would be. He knew many of the soldiers would need God, would wonder where God was amid such chaos, and possibly would lose their faith. So George made the decision to enlist. He wanted to be present for soldiers as they were being sent into combat to pray over them, to encourage them, and to answer their questions. He wanted to be present for the soldiers returning from missions, to sit with them in their shock and grief, and to hear their stories of trauma. And he wanted to be present for the soldiers killed in combat, to pray over them, to comfort their friends, and to offer words of solace to their families. George did all of this even though he does not believe there is any justification for violence or war and even though it cost him a great deal spiritually, emotionally, mentally, and physically. George knew he was God's beloved and couldn't help but live out that belovedness through faithful service to others. In doing so, I believe he has glorified God.

We all are not called to sign up to be military chaplains. But we all are called to serve God faithfully in some way because we are God's beloved. We find our call to live out our belovedness by being still. In the stillness, we experience true connection with God and begin to recognize who

God created us to be. We get in touch with our specific gifts and talents and passions. We draw on our belovedness, and from that place, we serve.

We run into problems with service because so many of us—myself included—find ourselves serving from a place of control, where we determine for ourselves our calling, who needs us, how to fulfill that need, and so on. To be sure, good things can come of that type of service. More often than not, however, that type of service is not sustainable. We run out of energy or inspiration. We may do more harm than good. Most importantly, we miss out on the experience of living out our true calling, a calling that is based solidly in our belovedness. Only from the quiet place where God affirms our belovedness do we find the inspiration, the assurance, the energy, and the joy we need to serve.

Allow me to offer a brief but important caveat: When speaking of service, it's important to note that I'm not saying we're beloved because we serve God. We cannot do anything to merit God's love. Instead, we are beloved first because God declares us so, whether we think we deserve it or not. Then, as we own our belovedness and live into it, we reflect God's love for the whole world as we serve others. When we live out of our belovedness, we won't be able to help it—we will feel compelled to serve.

This will have a glorious effect. When we serve as God's beloved, people around us will experience God's love through us. They will be drawn toward God and learn that they too are beloved. Then they can begin to live from that place of belovedness. They too will begin to serve, and God's name will be glorified again and again.

While all of this sounds lovely, the fact that servanthood may involve pain and sacrifice is not welcome news. We can see this in the reactions of the people surrounding Jesus. Some dismiss God's voice as thunder, while others assume angels are speaking solely to Jesus. The people don't understand—or don't want to understand—that the voice is directed at them and is for their benefit. God is trying to assure them that their acts of beloved service will not be in vain.

God speaks to us whether we are listening or not. God tries to reassure us whether we understand it or not. The more we practice stillness, the greater our ability to listen for and recognize God's voice of reassurance and deep love in our lives. The more we recognize God's naming us as beloved, the greater our ability to serve.

We are getting very close to the cross, which is distressing. The beloved journey is difficult, to be sure. But it is a journey to which we, God's beloved, are called. We are not alone on this journey; Jesus is with us. And we are not acting in vain; God's name will be glorified. God assures us of that. Thanks be to God. Amen.

REFLECTION QUESTIONS

1. What is significant about the Greeks showing up and asking for Jesus? What does it mean for you that Jesus' message is for all nations?

2. As Jesus talks about his impending death, what emotions do you hear in his voice? How does this make you feel?

3. What do you think God is trying to convey in speaking to Jesus and the people?

4. How is God calling you to beloved service? What does this service look like? How do you feel about this? What assurances is God offering you?

5. How does your view of service differ from God's view of service for you? Are you able to give up control in order to fulfill God's view of service? How will you glorify God's name by your service?

6. In what ways is God offering you reassurance?

7. How have you practiced stillness this week? What have you noticed?

PRAYER BEAD EXPERIENCE

Cross: Loving God,

Invitatory bead: who called your Beloved Son Jesus

Resurrection bead: to be a servant to the world,

1st cruciform bead: help me to follow Jesus, who was committed to living out his calling, no matter how painful.

Week beads, set 1: Use each bead to pay attention to Jesus' example of beloved service and to see yourself following Jesus.

2nd cruciform bead: Help me to live faithfully as your beloved servant.

Week beads, set 2: Use each bead to ask God for what you need to fulfill your calling in service to God.

3rd cruciform bead: Let my service bring you glory, O Lord.

Week beads, set 3: Use each bead to pray for the coming of God's glory through your service.

4th cruciform bead: Help me listen for your words of assurance.

Week beads, set 4: Use each bead to listen as God offers you assurance that God's name will be glorified through you.

Resurrection bead: In the name of Jesus Christ,

Invitatory bead: your Beloved Son,

Cross: Amen.

LISTENING MEDITATION

I am serving.

PALM
SUNDAY

BELOVED COURAGE

The next day the great crowd that had come for the festival heard that Jesus was coming to Jerusalem. They took palm branches and went out to meet him. They shouted, "Hosanna! *Blessings on the one who comes in the name of the Lord!* Blessings on the king of Israel!" Jesus found a young donkey and sat on it, just as it is written, *Don't be afraid, Daughter Zion. Look! Your king is coming, sitting on a donkey's colt.* His disciples didn't understand these things at first. After he was glorified, they remembered that these things had been written about him and that they had done these things to him.

—John 12:12–16 (CEB)

IT'S PALM SUNDAY, THE day we stand among the crowds in Jerusalem waving palm branches and shouting "Hosanna!" as Jesus rides humbly through the streets. But this day is bittersweet. By the end of this week, our shouts of "Hosanna!" will turn to demands that Jesus be crucified.

Reading this week and last week's scripture passages together points us to Jesus' courage. Jesus is afraid as he anticipates the excruciating pain that awaits him on the cross. As we noted last week, he wants to ask God to prevent this from happening. He wants to, but he doesn't. He intends to live out his calling no matter the price. That requires courage.

The word *courage* comes from the Latin *cor*, which means "heart." The original definition of courage was "telling the story of who you are with your whole heart." Jesus is God's Beloved Son; that is his story. He tells his story with his whole heart in the way he enters the city where he will be killed. Riding in on a stallion would have offered an impressive display of might. Instead, Jesus chooses to ride on a donkey—not a strong, mature donkey but a young colt. Jesus conveys his vulnerability to the crowd, the Romans, and the religious leaders who will soon turn on him. He exhibits true humility and expresses his commitment to peace. That is the story of who he is; that's what God's Beloved Son does. It's a true display of courage.

Verse 15 strikes me: "Don't be afraid, Daughter Zion. Look! Your king is coming, sitting on a donkey's colt." This verse is a reference to Zechariah 9:9, when the prophet Zechariah is trying to assure the nation of Israel that they will be saved from their enemies. "Don't be afraid!" he says before explaining that a king will ride in on a donkey's colt. If I'd been living in fear for the safety of my people, I'm not sure that news would comfort me. A donkey's colt? Are you sure? How is someone riding on an immature donkey going to protect and defend me? How will that person be able to overcome my enemies?

But riding into Jerusalem as Jesus did, completely vulnerable to his enemies, is different from a ruler riding into conflict perched on a stallion, wearing armor, carrying weapons, and surrounded by warriors. While such a ruler may be brave, Jesus' entrance requires true courage. His courage is not derived from a big horse or battle gear but from an internal place of deep conviction. His courage originates from his belovedness, his identity in God. That's the type of savior I need and want. It's also the type of person I want and need to be for myself. I need to be courageous. I need to be in touch with my truth so that I'm willing and able to tell the story of my belovedness with my whole heart through my words, actions, and presence. Such authenticity connects me to God and helps me to be my truest self.

When I'm acting courageously by living into my calling as exactly the person God created me to be, I find my strength, passion, inspiration, and motivation.

Even so, I don't always live courageously, and I know I'm not alone. We often give up on ourselves because we believe we aren't enough: not strong enough, not smart enough, not pretty enough, not talented enough, not good enough. When we give up on ourselves, we stop speaking the truth of our belovedness and instead live out of our insecurities, fears, and need for control.

From Jesus riding through Jerusalem, we learn that vulnerability lies at the heart of courage. That may not seem to make sense—how can we be vulnerable and courageous? But all along our journey, Jesus has been showing us that vulnerability is vital. The way of the beloved is stillness, which fosters true connection with God. Stillness requires vulnerability. In stillness we let go of our need for control and acknowledge the only one who is really in control: God. We can just be. We don't have to be good at prayer or a good Christian; we don't have to be happy or smart; we don't have to be successful or good at sports. We can just be. And when we can just be, we learn to rely on God for everything, from our identity to our way of being in the world. The vulnerability of stillness facilitates that divine connection we're searching for.

During the first session of my cohort of The Upper Room's Two-Year Academy for Spiritual Formation, Elizabeth Canham, an Episcopal priest and one of the faculty members, taught me a new way of praying Psalm 46:10. By breaking it down, she explained, we would not only develop a rhythmic meditation but also increase our understanding of the verse's meaning.

Be still, and know that I am God.
Be still, and know that I am.
Be still, and know.
Be still.
Be.

This way of the praying the psalm was striking. I've always loved this verse and have it displayed in many forms around my house and studio. Now I heard it in a new way. What does it mean to know God: the Lord, the Giver of Life, the Creator of the Universe? What does it mean to know I AM (as God says to Moses in Exodus 3:14): that God exists, has always existed, and will always exist? What does it mean to know—really know? What does it mean to be still? And, finally, what does it mean to be? I began to recite this litany over and over during my prayer time and throughout the day.

When I arrived for the final session of the Academy in May 2014, one of my friends, Sally Nettles, had made laminated bookmarks for each member of the cohort as a parting gift. Printed on the bookmark was the breakdown of Psalm 46:10 as Rev. Canham had taught us, but Sally had added two more lines:

Beloved.
Be love.

When we can just be—when we can let go of everything and be completely vulnerable with God, we will hear that we are beloved. The longer and more often we sit in the stillness and own our belovedness, the more we will realize we cannot keep this to ourselves. We will be compelled to share this news of belovedness with the world, to help others hear that they too are beloved. We will be love. No matter the cost.

It's no accident that the closer we get to the cross the more we need to talk about courage and vulnerability. With every step in our journey, Jesus becomes increasingly more vulnerable. Today he is riding toward the place of his death on a young colt. Later this week, we will watch him wash the feet of his disciples, eat dinner with the people who will betray him, and rebuke Peter for trying to defend him against the guards sent to arrest him. We will observe Jesus refusing to argue with Pilate for his freedom, submitting to torture, and dragging his own cross up to Golgotha. And we will stand at the foot of the cross and watch helplessly as he dies the death of a common criminal while carrying the weight of our sins and shame on his shoulders. It doesn't get more vulnerable or more courageous than that. This too is the way of the beloved.

We are called to live into our belovedness with courage. At times we will be called to take risks and make sacrifices. We will be called to be vulnerable and lean into uncertainty and even fear. We will be called to do what is necessary to glorify God. It may be scary, and it will require a great deal of courage. But it will be possible because we will be living out our true story with our whole heart. And it will be possible because Jesus sends his Spirit so that we too might live this life of belovedness.

What does it look like to live with courage? How can we discern the ways in which God is calling us to live out our truth? Some of us may not know the answers to these questions yet, and that's okay. This is only a seven-week study, and the process of healing and owning our belovedness takes time. So we must be patient and offer ourselves time. We must continue to return to the stillness, where we will meet the Jesus who is living into his courage so that we will know once and for all just how deeply we are loved.

REFLECTION QUESTIONS

1. How do you think Jesus feels as he rides through the streets of Jerusalem? What is significant about Jesus' riding on a donkey's colt?

2. In what ways do you see Jesus displaying courage in this story? What connections do you see between vulnerability and courage?

3. What do you make of Zechariah 9:9?

4. What are the connections between having courage and understanding your belovedness?

5. Think of a time when you lived courageously. Now think of a time when you lived from a place of insecurity and fear. What was different about these two experiences? How did each one make you feel? How did you handle each situation? What were the outcomes? What do these outcomes tell you?

6. In what ways does being beloved give you courage? How does practicing stillness feed your courage and your sense of being beloved? In what ways or in what areas of your life is God calling you to display courage?

7. How have you practiced stillness this week? What have you noticed?

Prayer Bead Experience

Cross: God of love,

Invitatory bead: whose Son, Jesus,

Resurrection bead: is a model of courage,

1st cruciform bead: I watch as Jesus enters Jerusalem in faithfulness to your calling.

Week beads, set 1: Use each bead to watch Jesus as he processes through the city. What do you notice?

2nd cruciform bead: Although he is afraid and vulnerable, Jesus exhibits courage.

Week beads, set 2: Use each bead to focus on Jesus' courage. What are signs of his courage?

3rd cruciform bead: As your beloved, I know that I too will need to act with courage as I live into my calling.

Week beads, set 3: Use each bead to recognize the ways and times in which you may need to act with courage as you live out your calling.

4th cruciform bead: Help me to rely on you for courage, knowing you will always be with me.

Week beads, set 4: Use each bead to pray for courage.

Resurrection bead: In the name of Jesus Christ,

Invitatory bead: the Beloved.

Cross: Amen.

LISTENING MEDITATION

I am courageous.

GOOD
FRIDAY

BELOVED DOUBT

At daybreak, the chief priests—with the
elders, legal experts, and the whole Sanhe-
drin—formed a plan. They bound Jesus, led
him away, and turned him over to Pilate.
Pilate questioned him, "Are you the king of
the Jews?" Jesus replied, "That's what you
say." The chief priests were accusing him of
many things. Pilate asked him again, "Aren't
you going to answer? What about all these
accusations?" But Jesus gave no more answers,
so that Pilate marveled. During the festival,
Pilate released one prisoner to them, whom-
ever they requested. A man named Barabbas
was locked up with the rebels who had committed murder during an uprising. The crowd
pushed forward and asked Pilate to release

someone, as he regularly did. Pilate answered them, "Do you want me to release to you the king of the Jews?" He knew that the chief priests had handed him over because of jealousy. But the chief priests stirred up the crowd to have him release Barabbas to them instead. Pilate replied, "Then what do you want me to do with the one you call king of the Jews?" They shouted back, "Crucify him!" Pilate said to them, "Why? What wrong has he done?" They shouted even louder, "Crucify him!" Pilate wanted to satisfy the crowd, so he released Barabbas to them. He had Jesus whipped, then handed him over to be crucified.

The soldiers led Jesus away into the courtyard of the palace known as the governor's headquarters, and they called together the whole company of soldiers. They dressed him up in a purple robe and twisted together a crown of thorns and put it on him. They saluted him, "Hey! King of the Jews!" Again and again, they struck his head with a stick. They spit on him and knelt before him to honor him. When they finished mocking him, they stripped him of the purple robe and put his own clothes back on him. Then they led him out to crucify him.

Simon, a man from Cyrene, Alexander and Rufus' father, was coming in from the countryside. They forced him to carry his cross. They brought Jesus to the place called Golgotha, which means Skull Place. They tried to give him wine mixed with myrrh, but he didn't take it. They crucified him. They divided up his clothes, drawing lots for them to determine who would take what. It was nine in the morning when they crucified him. The notice of the formal charge against him was written, "The king of the Jews." They crucified two outlaws with him, one on his right and one on his left. People walking by insulted him, shaking their heads and saying, "Ha! So you were going to destroy the temple and rebuild it in three days, were you? Save yourself and come down from that cross!" In the same way, the chief priests were making fun of him among themselves, together with the legal experts. "He saved others," they said, "but he can't save himself. Let the Christ, the king of Israel, come down from the cross.

Then we'll see and believe." Even those who had been crucified with Jesus insulted him.

From noon until three in the afternoon the whole earth was dark. At three, Jesus cried out with a loud shout, "*Eloi, eloi, lama sabachthani*," which means, "My God, my God, why have you left me?"

After hearing him, some standing there said, "Look! He's calling Elijah!" Someone ran, filled a sponge with sour wine, and put it on a pole. He offered it to Jesus to drink, saying, "Let's see if Elijah will come to take him down." But Jesus let out a loud cry and died. The curtain of the sanctuary was torn in two from top to bottom. When the centurion, who stood facing Jesus, saw how he died, he said, "This man was certainly God's Son." Some women were watching from a distance, including Mary Magdalene and Mary the mother of James (the younger one) and Joses, and Salome. When Jesus was in Galilee, these women had followed and supported him, along with many other women who had come to Jerusalem with him.

Since it was late in the afternoon on Preparation Day, just before the Sabbath, Joseph of

Arimathea dared to approach Pilate and ask for Jesus' body. (Joseph was a prominent council member who also eagerly anticipated the coming of God's kingdom.) Pilate wondered if Jesus was already dead. He called the centurion and asked him whether Jesus had already died. When he learned from the centurion that Jesus was dead, Pilate gave the dead body to Joseph. He bought a linen cloth, took Jesus down from the cross, wrapped him in the cloth, and laid him in a tomb that had been carved out of rock. He rolled a stone against the entrance to the tomb. Mary Magdalene and Mary the mother of Joses saw where he was buried.

—Mark 15:1-47 (CEB)

IT IS GOOD FRIDAY, the day Jesus is mocked, tortured, and crucified. Our journey has led to this moment.

To enter into the meaning and mood of this day, I provided the entire length of Mark 15 so that we can read everything that happens on Good Friday. Even though we may be familiar with this passage, let's read through it slowly and carefully again. Once finished, spend some time sitting quietly. Consider our journey: where we started, where we've traveled, how we have learned we are beloved, and what it means for our lives. Consider how we got to this moment of gut-wrenching pain. Hear Jesus' mournful cry on the cross: "My God, my God, why have you left me?"

We are beloved. We are called to lives of wonder, listening, healing, passion, service, and courage. But we will have times of doubt when we question whether we really are God's beloved. When the world is shrouded in darkness, we may question whether God is present at all. We may think, *Perhaps God has abandoned me.* When pain is everywhere, we may wonder, *Where is God in this? Am I alone?*

It is easy to rush toward Easter. Yet Good Friday invites us to sit with our pain and questions and grief. Holy Saturday provides space to sit in the emptiness and darkness and wonder whether we will see light again.

After spending time with our own pain and questions and with Jesus' pain and questions, may we consider the listening meditation today and tomorrow. I intentionally did not include a prayer bead experience, preferring to focus on as few words as possible in this space of questioning. Let's focus on the listening meditation, praying it with our prayer beads, repeating it as we walk or drive or do the dishes, or saying it to ourselves as we lie in bed at night. May we notice our doubts, pain, and grief; and, in doing so, may we connect with Jesus and his followers' doubts, pain, and grief.

LISTENING MEDITATION

Am I beloved?

EASTER

BELOVED WITNESS

Early in the morning of the first day of the week, while it was still dark, Mary Magdalene came to the tomb and saw that the stone had been taken away from the tomb. She ran to Simon Peter and the other disciple, the one whom Jesus loved, and said, "They have taken the Lord from the tomb, and we don't know where they've put him." Peter and the other disciple left to go to the tomb. They were running together, but the other disciple ran faster than Peter and was the first to arrive at the tomb. Bending down to take a look, he saw the linen cloths lying there, but he didn't go in. Following him, Simon Peter entered the tomb and saw the linen cloths lying there. He also saw the face cloth that had been on Jesus' head. It wasn't with the other clothes but was folded up in its own place. Then the other disciple, the one who arrived at the tomb first, also went inside. He saw and believed. They didn't yet understand the scripture that Jesus must rise from the dead. Then the disciples returned to the place where they were staying.

Mary stood outside near the tomb, crying. As she cried, she bent down to look into the tomb. She saw two angels dressed in white, seated where the body of Jesus had been, one at the head and one at the foot. The angels asked her, "Woman, why are you crying?"

She replied, "They have taken away my Lord, and I don't know where they've put him." As soon as she had said this, she turned around and saw Jesus standing there, but she didn't know it was Jesus. Jesus said to her, "Woman, why are you crying? Who are you looking for?" Thinking he was the gardener, she replied, "Sir, if you have carried him away, tell me where you have put him and I will get him." Jesus said to her, "Mary." She turned and said to him in Aramaic, "Rabbouni" (which means *Teacher*).

Jesus said to her, "Don't hold on to me, for I haven't yet gone up to my Father. Go to my brothers and sisters and tell them, 'I'm going up to my Father and your Father, to my God and your God.'" Mary Magdalene left and announced to the disciples, "I've seen the Lord." Then she told them what he said to her.

—John 20:1-18 (CEB)

ALLELUIA! CHRIST IS RISEN!

Our journey has led us to an empty tomb. There is no more joyful destination than this. It is a place of resurrection: Jesus, God's Beloved Son, has risen from the dead.

This means so much for us, my fellow journeyers. It means we are so beloved that Jesus died so that we might be saved from sin and death. It means we are so beloved that God offers us the gift of eternal life. God loves us so much that God wants to be with us always. It means our belovedness is more powerful than our doubt and our own self-rejection; God's love proves stronger.

Our journey does not end here. So much awaits us. Jesus calls us to follow Mary, who runs to tell the others that Christ is risen. By following in her footsteps, we will share the truth of our belovedness and help others connect with theirs. That is our witness: We are *all* beloved. That is how we can be love.

The journey will not always be easy. We may find ourselves in places of doubt, believing we are not beloved. But those places are never dead ends. Those are the points in our path where God is most present for us—whether we know it or not—and where God is guiding us forward. The way of the beloved always leads to a greater, richer, deeper sense of our belovedness.

As we continue in our beloved journey, may we continue to practice stillness and use the prayer practices we've learned together. They will help us slow down long enough to hear God's voice of deep love in our lives. They will help us connect with the source of our wonder, passion, healing, service, and courage. They will get us through the times of doubt. They will lead us to places and times of witness.

We are God's beloved. That is our truth. May God continue to bless us along the journey as we live into this truth.

Alleluia! Christ is risen!

PRAYER BEAD EXPERIENCE

Cross: God of love,

Invitatory bead: alleluia!

Resurrection bead: Christ is risen!

1ˢᵗ cruciform bead: I rejoice at the resurrection of your Son, Jesus Christ.

Week beads, set 1: Use each bead to rejoice at Christ's resurrection.

2ⁿᵈ cruciform bead: You have saved me from sin and death because you love me so much, and I am grateful.

Week beads, set 2: Use each bead to offer gratitude to God for the gift of eternal life.

3ʳᵈ cruciform bead: As your beloved, help me to share the news of your love to all I meet.

Week beads, set 3: Use each bead to ask God to guide you in sharing the news of Christ's resurrection.

4ᵗʰ cruciform bead: I am your beloved, Lord. This is my truth!

Week beads, set 4: Use each bead to affirm and own your beloved truth.

Resurrection bead: In the name of Jesus Christ,

Invitatory bead: the Beloved.

Cross: Amen.

LISTENING MEDITATION

I am beloved! You are beloved!

LEADER'S GUIDE

IF YOU AND YOUR group members will be making your own prayer beads in the first session along with discussing the introduction of the book, I suggest allowing for one-and-a-half to two hours of meeting time. To maximize your time together, review the instructions on making prayer beads on pages 111–120 beforehand. Prior to the bead-making session, consider watching the instructional video found at http://prayerworksstudio.com/prayer-beads/make-your-own/. Better yet, by making a set of prayer beads in advance, you ensure your ability to lead group members through this activity and have a sample set to show them. If you and your group members are not making beads, you can discuss the introductory material at the Week One meeting. One hour is sufficient for the rest of the weekly meetings. As the study leader, plan to arrive fifteen minutes early to prepare the meeting space.

I recommend arranging chairs around a table so that group members are facing one another. This arrangement will facilitate dialogue as well as allow space for books, prayer beads, and notes. If a round table is not available, arrange chairs in a circle.

I also encourage you to think about ways to create a prayerful mood in the meeting room. Perhaps you can light a candle and play soft instrumental music in the background as members arrive or set up a small worship center with a cross, icon, and/or Bible. There is no need to make this complicated; simple settings often lend themselves to a spirit of contemplation, reflection, and prayer.

INTRODUCTORY OPENING

Since this will be the first time for people to meet (unless they met previously to make prayer beads), take time to welcome each participant. Then, allow each person to introduce himself or herself. As part of the introductions, invite participants to do the following:

- show their prayer beads to the group. Encourage them to talk about the beads: Did they make the set? If so, how did they choose the colors or design? What was meaningful about the process of making the set? If they did not make the prayer beads, where did they get them? Why did they choose that particular set? Was it given to them as a gift?

- share what drew them to this study. How did they hear about the study? What about the study interested them? Have they prayed with beads before?
- raise questions related to what they hope to receive from this study. What are they wanting to learn?

Next, orient the group members to the study. Ask if anyone had specific questions about the introduction. Then, review the study outline. The study takes place over seven weeks, from Ash Wednesday to Palm Sunday. Each week includes a scripture passage, a weekly reading, reflection questions, a prayer bead experience, and a listening meditation. The prayer bead experiences and listening meditations offer two different ways for participants to use their prayer beads (though they are welcome to practice these prayers without beads).

You may point out that the study also includes two additional lessons—one for Good Friday and one for Easter—in which the formats differ slightly. These two lessons are intended to be read individually rather than with the group.

For the weekly study, encourage the participants to do the following:

- take 30–45 minutes each week to read the assigned scripture passage and weekly reading;
- write down any insights or questions they may have and bring them to the study meetings;

- review responses to the reflection questions; and
- spend at least five minutes each day using the prayer bead experience and/or the listening meditation.

Following this weekly routine will ensure that each participant will benefit as much as possible from the study.

Assure the participants that there are no right or wrong ways to use prayer beads. This study introduces people to two ways to use beads in prayer and gives participants an opportunity to experiment using the prayer bead experiences and listening meditations. Some of the experiences may be more comfortable or compelling than others, and that is okay. The experiences may inspire participants to come up with their own ways of using beads in prayer. Ultimately, the beads are intended to help people quiet their minds and draw closer to God. Hopefully, the beads will help them gain a certain comfort level with prayer, experience God in a new way, and recognize they are God's beloved.

In closing, ask the group members to hold their prayer beads in their hands. Explain that you will bless the beads using the following prayer:

> God of love, you love us enough to call us into your presence through prayer, and for that we give thanks.
>
> We thank you for the many ways in which we can connect with you, including through the use of prayer beads.

We ask your blessing upon these beads. May they remind us of your loving presence, draw us into prayer, focus our time with you, and help us to listen as you call us "beloved."

We pray this in the name of Jesus, your Beloved Son. Amen.

WEEKLY FORMAT

OPENING

When all participants have arrived and found a seat, take a moment to help them transition from the noise and rush of daily life to this time of reflection and discussion. Encourage participants to hold their prayer beads, close their eyes, and take three deep breaths. This does not have to be formal; let it be an opportunity to relax and be still in God's presence.

PRAYING

Each week, identify one person as the leader. The leader will read the prayer bead experience aloud while participants hold their prayer beads and follow along with each bead. When the leader comes to the cruciform bead, he or she will read the prayer for that bead aloud, allowing time for silence as the participants pray silently while fingering each of the seven week beads. After providing a sufficient amount of time for the participants to pray with all seven week beads (about one minute), the leader will read aloud the prayer for the next cruciform bead. Continue in this way through the conclusion of the prayer. Another option is to invite participants to pray the listening meditation with their prayer beads. Again, allow sufficient time for participants to pray silently through the full set of prayer beads (about three minutes).

READING

After a volunteer reads the scripture aloud, invite the group members to take a moment for prayerful consideration of the scripture, or you can say, "The Word of God for the people of God." They would respond by saying, "Thanks be to God." Then invite participants to share any thoughts or insights they received while listening.

REVIEWING

You may choose to review each question in order. Read it aloud, and allow time for the group members' responses. Another option is to invite group members to speak about the questions they found most thought-provoking.

The challenge in working with groups comes in finding a balance between the extroverts and the introverts.

Inevitably, you will have members who are talkative and feel comfortable speaking in groups while others are shy, quiet, or need more time to process their thoughts. It is important to create an environment in which every participant feels encouraged and comfortable to share if he or she chooses without putting undue pressure on those who prefer to remain silent. If you find yourself leading a group that is unusually quiet, experiment with ways of encouraging each member to participate. Perhaps you could ask the members to take turns reading and/or responding to the question aloud.

SHARING

Encourage participants to share their thoughts and observations from the prayer bead experience. Ask how the experience helped in their understanding of being God's beloved.

CLOSING

Choose one of the following options:

- invite participants to pray through the listening meditation for that week, if you haven't done so in a group already; or
- invite someone to offer a closing prayer.

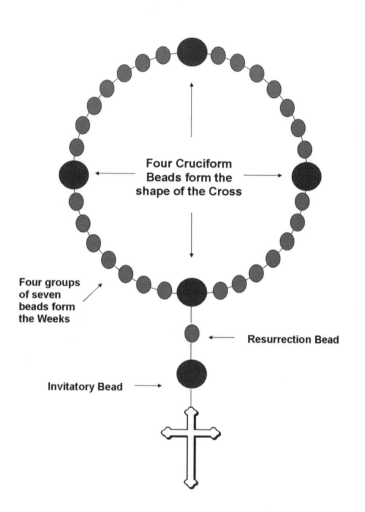

Four Cruciform Beads form the shape of the Cross

Four groups of seven beads form the Weeks

Resurrection Bead

Invitatory Bead

Introduction to Protestant Prayer Beads

The way of the beloved is stillness: learning to quiet our minds so we can hear God call us beloved. Prayer beads, then, are one piece of equipment for the journey; they help us reduce the noise in our minds, relax our bodies, increase our focus, and experience God's presence.

While many types of prayer beads exist, I designed the prayer bead experiences and listening meditations in this book for use with Protestant prayer beads. Many Protestants are unfamiliar with this form of prayer beads; they generally are more familiar with the beads used by Catholics to pray the rosary. These two forms of prayer beads certainly have some common history, evolving as a way for Christians to "pray continually" (1 Thess. 5:17). Though the rosary is more than one thousand years old, a group of Episcopalians in Texas developed Protestant prayer beads in the 1980s. The group wanted to reclaim ancient prayer practices, and after meeting for a period of time, they created the "Anglican rosary," a form of prayer beads for Protestant use.

While sixty beads make up the rosary, Protestant prayer beads are made up of a cross or other pendant and thirty-three or more beads. One large bead, called the "invitatory bead," reminds us that God invites us to a time of prayer. We may use this bead to begin our prayer, much like churches employ a call to worship to begin a church service.

In addition to the large invitatory bead, Protestant prayer beads include four more large beads. When we splay out a set of Protestant prayer beads, these beads form the four points of a cross and thus are called "cruciform beads."

Between each of the cruciform beads is a set of seven smaller beads. Because a week has seven days, these beads are called "week beads." The number 7 has bountiful meaning for Christians:

- The church calendar consists of seven seasons (Advent, Christmas, Epiphany, Lent, Easter, Pentecost, and Ordinary Time).
- Genesis tells us there were seven days of creation; on the seventh day, God rested, calling us to keep it holy.
- The number 7 shows up often in the book of Revelation, including John's note that his letter is addressed to the "seven churches" (1:4).
- Both Jews and Christians believe the number 7 symbolizes spiritual perfection.

When we add together the one invitatory bead, the four cruciform beads, and the twenty-eight week beads, we get a total of thirty-three beads. (See diagram on page 106.) The group that developed this format appreciated this number since it represented Jesus' life on earth for thirty-three years.

As I explain in my first book, *A Bead and a Prayer: A Beginner's Guide to Protestant Prayer Beads*, for the first year I chose to use that number of beads. However, over time I realized I wanted some representation of the fact that Christ still lives today, particularly since the Resurrection is the hallmark of the Christian faith. So I added one more bead, positioning it between the invitatory bead and the bottom cruciform bead. I call it the "resurrection bead" and use it in my prayers to focus on Christ's gift to us of eternal life. Adding this bead makes the total number of beads thirty-four. However, I still tell people that Protestant prayer beads are comprised of thirty-three beads, which represent Jesus' life and ministry on earth—plus one bead to represent his resurrection.

I want to emphasize that there is no right or wrong way to make prayer beads. This study will focus on the Protestant prayer bead format of thirty-four beads; however, participants may design their own format as I did and modify the devotions accordingly. Since this is an individual prayer tool, it should be meaningful for each person and his or her time with God.

Like the rosary, Protestant prayer beads offer various benefits to prayer: They enhance focus, offer a way of being still, and serve as a sign of God's presence. But whereas the rosary has a formula for prayers to be said with each bead, Protestant prayer beads do not. This means we can use them in any way that feels comfortable and even experiment with different ways of using them, depending upon our need at the time. Consider this a wonderful opportunity to explore new ways of being with God.

MAKING PROTESTANT PRAYER BEADS[5]

MAKING A SET OF prayer beads is fairly easy, even if you have no prior beading experience. If you haven't already, consider watching the instructional video found at http://prayerworksstudio.com/prayer-beads/make-your-own/.

APPROACHES AND SKILL LEVELS

- If you have plenty of time for the bead-making session, I recommend purchasing beads in a variety of colors and allowing the participants to create their own designs. This approach can encourage people to give thought to the color and composition of this prayer tool.

- If you have limited time, I suggest you prepare "kits" in advance. Each kit would contain all the materials one person would need to complete a set of prayer beads, except for the tools and crimp tubes. You might offer some variety among the kits—such as two or three different color combinations—to allow for some choice and individualization.

You will also want to consider the participants' *skill level* when it comes to working with beads.

- If you have one or two *experienced participants* who have worked with beads and the rest have *little or no background*, I recommend that you attach the crosses to the wire ahead of time (see step 1, page 116). This saves time and frustration and makes the prayer-bead-making session much more enjoyable.
- If you are working with a group of *skilled beaders,* they may feel quite capable of attaching the cross to the wire themselves.

In addition to the beads, I recommend having a small bowl or tray for each participant to collect his or her beads or to hold the kit as the prayer beads are assembled.

The Crimp Tubes

Successful completion of prayer beads is due, in large part, to the crimp tubes. Although tiny, these tubes serve a critical function in the formation of the prayer beads. Allow me to stress three aspects:

1. Distribute the crimp tubes separately from the other prayer bead materials. The reason for this is simple: The tiny crimp tubes can easily get lost if mixed with a larger bag or bowl of beads. Whether I use preassembled kits or allow participants to choose their own beads, I always pass out the crimp tubes myself, carefully placing them in front of the participants and drawing their attention to them. It might help to assign a crimp-tube distributor.

2. Make sure participants understand the placement of the crimp tubes on their wires. They must add the crimp tubes to the wire early in the process rather than adding them later. If someone strings all the beads on the wire and realizes he or she has forgotten to add the crimp tube, that person will have to undo the set and start all over.

3. Be prepared to provide assistance to participants who need help threading the crimp tubes onto the wire. Again, you might consider having someone who distributes and provides assistance with the crimp tubes.

THE TOOLS

A crucial component to making prayer beads is the tools. The good news is that beading requires only two tools: chain nose pliers and side wire cutters. The even better news is that you can find both of these tools at a craft store, a hardware store, or in your family's toolbox. If you have no beading experience, I encourage you to practice using the tools before leading the group through this activity.

I recommend that you identify one person to be in charge of "tying off " the prayer beads. (If you have more than one person who can do this, all the better.) This person sits at a table with the tools. As participants finish stringing their beads together, they can bring their sets to the tool person. The tool person can then complete steps 13–14.

ROOM SETUP

Making prayer beads can be a good group-building activity. People seem to enjoy talking and bonding with one another as they string their beads. I recommend using round or rectangular tables where people can sit facing one another. If that is not possible, a classroom or training room setup will work as well.

At the front, side, or back of the room, set up a table where you can lay out all of the bead-making supplies or kits. This may be the same table where the identified tool person sits to tie off the prayer beads.

Consider adding other enhancements to this experience, such as

- a music player available to play Taizé or other soft background music;
- completed sets of prayer beads around the room for people to see; and
- snacks or beverages.

MATERIALS AND TOOLS NEEDED

The materials listed below can be purchased at a local craft store. My company, Prayerworks Studio, offers kits, which include the necessary materials. We also offer the tools for sale. You may purchase the kits and tools at www.prayer worksstudio.etsy.com. Use the discount code BOOK20 to receive 20 percent off your purchase.

- 5 large (10mm–12mm) beads
- 29 medium (8mm–10mm) beads
- 36 seed (size #6 or #8) beads
- 1 cross or other pendant
- 2 crimp tubes (size 2 x 2)
- 20–24 inches of wire (49 strand, .18 or .19 inches)
- 1 pair of chain nose pliers
- 1 set of side wire cutters

INSTRUCTIONS

L = Large bead (cruciform and invitatory) M = Medium bead (week and resurrection) S = seed bead

STEP 1: Thread one of the crimp tubes onto the wire, then add the cross. (See figure 1.) Thread the end of the wire back up through the crimp tube. This will leave you with the two ends of the wire coming out of the crimp tube: the primary length of wire and a smaller "tail," about one inch in length. Using the pliers, squeeze the crimp tube until it is flattened. (See figure 2.)

Figure 1

STEP 2: String the beads in the following pattern, taking them all the way down so that the first bead aligns with the crimp tube that sits above the cross (Note: Make sure the beads cover both wires—the primary wire and the extra piece that extends from the top of the cross):

s L s M s L s

Figure 2

STEP 3: String the crimp tube (*this is a critical step!*).

STEP 4: String the first section of week beads in the following pattern: s M (7 times), then 1 s. It will look like this:

s M s M s M s M s M s M s M s

STEP 5: String 1 L bead.

STEP 6: String the second section of week beads by repeating step 4.

STEP 7: String 1 L bead.

STEP 8: String the third section of week beads by repeating step 4.

STEP 9: String 1 L bead.

STEP 10: String the fourth section of week beads by repeating step 4.

STEP 11: Take the end of the wire and thread it back through the crimp tube that was added in step 3 (the wire will be heading back toward the cross; see figure 3).Thread it through the crimp tube, the seed bead, the large bead, the seed bead, and the medium bead so that it comes out from the bottom of the medium bead.

Figure 3

STEP 12: Pull the wire tightly, adjusting the beads as necessary to remove any slack in the wire and to ensure that the wire is completely covered up by the beads (figure 4). This is a good time to count all the beads and double check your pattern to be sure the beads are in the order you desire. If not, make the necessary changes before proceeding to the next step.

Figure 4

STEP 13: Using a pair of chain nose pliers, flatten the crimp tube as tightly as possible.

STEP 14: Using a set of side wire cutters, cut the remaining wire off as close to the beads as possible.

Completed Set

Enjoy your beads! Blessings!

*All prayer bead instruction photos are courtesy of Blanka Gresham.

Writing Your Own Prayer Bead Experience

As you begin your beloved journey, I invite you to write your own prayer bead experience. Doing so offers you an opportunity to consider where you are in your spiritual journey and how you might share it with God. Are you listening for God to call you beloved, or are you in the wilderness, struggling to believe you are beloved? Are you wondering, listening, healing, serving, or witnessing? Are you in the midst of passion, courage, or doubt? Wherever you are, think about what you want to say to God or hear from God. Your words may change along the way, so consider copying this template and creating as many forms of your own devotion as you want. Additionally, carry one listening meditation with you throughout your journey, or write a new one for each day, week, or month.

As always, there is no wrong way to pray. No matter what you say or how you go about it, you will be blessed in your desire to connect with God. And you will be reminded of your belovedness.

PRAYER BEAD EXPERIENCE

Cross:

Invitatory bead:

Resurrection bead:

1st cruciform bead:

Week beads, set 1:

2nd cruciform bead:

Week beads, set 2:

3rd cruciform bead:

Week beads, set 3:

4th cruciform bead:

Week beads, set 4:

Resurrection bead:

Invitatory bead:

Cross: Amen.

LISTENING MEDITATION

Notes

1. Father Richard Rohr, OFM, "God's Self-Revelation," Center for Action and Contemplation, Sunday, January 14, 2018, https://cac.org/gods-self-revelation-2018-01-14/.
2. Rohr, "God's Self-Revelation."
3. Matt Skinner, "Commentary on Matthew 6:1-6, 16-21," Working Preacher, February 25, 2009, https://www.workingpreacher.org/preaching.aspx?commentary_id=252.
4. Henri J. M. Nouwen, *Life of the Beloved: Spiritual Living in a Secular World* (New York: The Crossroad Publishing Company, 1992), 33.
5. Excerpted from Kristen E. Vincent's *Another Bead, Another Prayer: Devotions to Use with Protestant Prayer Beads* (Nashville, TN: Upper Room Books, 2014), 105–15.

ACKNOWLEDGMENTS

MANY PEOPLE HAVE JOURNEYED with me, both in writing this book and in helping me discover my own belovedness:

- the folks who participated in my *Beloved Journey* eCourse, which led to the content for this book: Kathleen, Claire, Ashley, Barbara (hi, Mom!), Janet, Anna, Joli, Phyllis, Ramona, Lynne, Walter, and Jeri Lynn;

- my beloved editors, Erin Palmer and Joanna Bradley Kennedy, who loved this book into being with their thoughtful input, gracious wordsmithing, and ongoing encouragement;

- everyone involved in The Academy for Spiritual Formation, the place where I first learned the way of the beloved and began to own my belovedness;

- the good people of St. James United Methodist Church, who have graciously welcomed my family into theirs and who help me experience my belovedness a little more each day; and

- Max and Matthew, who are the clearest and most immediate reminders that God loves me deeply.

About the Author

KRISTEN E. VINCENT IS passionate about helping people recognize, own, and revel in God's deep love for them. She does this by writing award-winning books, leading retreats, and making prayer beads. She also works with soldiers and others who have PTSD and travels internationally to help communities heal from widespread trauma, so they can remember their belovedness.

Kristen is the author of five books including *A Bead and a Prayer: A Beginner's Guide to Protestant Prayer Beads* and *Beads of Healing: Prayer, Trauma, and Spiritual Wholeness*. She has a Master of Theological Studies from Duke Divinity School and is a graduate of The Academy for Spiritual Formation (#34). She is married to Max, a United Methodist pastor; their son, Matthew, is a budding rock guitarist. Kristen loves dark chocolate, the color indigo, and people in T-Rex costumes. She is making good progress in her lifelong quest for the perfect chocolate mousse recipe.

Every Tuesday, Kristen sends out a Loved Note by email. Loved Notes are designed to remind people that they are deeply loved (get it? *Loved Notes*!) by God. There's nothing else to them—no sales pitches or other marketing gimmicks. They simply are short notes to remind you of your belovedness. If you would like to subscribe—or for more information on Kristen and her work—visit prayerworksstudio.com.